Global Environmental Change:

Deforestation

National Science Teachers Association

NSTA's *Global Environmental Change* series is science based, and links the ecology and biology of global environmental changes with insights and information from other disciplines. The series teaches students how to gather a wide range of relevant data and information derived from pertinent areas of study, and encourages them to pose and then answer their own questions in order to make their own decisions about solving global environmental problems.

Deforestation is the second installment in the *Global Environmental Change* series, which the National Science Teachers Association created in conjunction with the U.S. Environmental Protection Agency's Office of Research and Development. Other installments also use case studies to focus on such global environmental topics as biodiversity, inrtoduced species, and carrying capacity.

The National Science Teachers Association, founded in 1944 and headquartered in Arlington, Virginia, is the largest organization in the world committed to the improvement of science education at all levels—preschool through college.

ACKNOWLEDGMENTS

Deforestation's contributors included Margaret Edwards, Irwin Slesnick, Frank Ireton, Linda Wygoda, and Brad Williamson. The series was developed by: Ron Slotkin, EPA Office of Research and Development; Shirley Watt Ireton, NSTA Special Publications, Managing Editor; Gregg Sekscienski, NSTA Special Publications, former Associate Editor; and Margaret Edwards, writer. Jim Sproull and Roy Q. Beven lent experience and guidance to its development. Ongoing support for the *Global Environmental Change* series is provided by the U.S. Environmental Protection Agency's Office of Research and Development.

Deforestation was published by NSTA—Gerry Wheeler, Executive Director; and Phyllis Marcuccio, Associate Executive Director for Publications—and produced by NSTA Special Publications—Shirley Watt Ireton, Managing Editor; Chris Findlay, Associate Editor; Doug Messier, Associate Editor; Jocelyn Lofstrom, Assistant Editor; Eric Knaub, Program Assistant; and Christina Frasch, Editorial Assistant. Chris Findlay was Project Editor. *Deforestation* was designed by Donna Lomangino, Inc. David Miller was the principal artist. The cover was designed by Marty Ittner of Auras Design.

The cover photograph was taken by Kathleen Norris Cook. The back cover map inset is from Digial Wisdom, Inc.'s Mountain High Maps and Globeshots CD-ROM. The back cover erosion inset is provided courtesy of the EPA. The back cover inset of school children on a tree branch is from Images, copyright © 1996 PhotoDisc, Inc. The topographic map and aerial photograph on page 14 appears courtesy of Western Washington State University; the 1995 photograph was taken by Lori McGriff Boroughs and appears courtesy of Western Washington State University.

PB138X02
ISBN : 0-87355-158-3
Library of Congress Card Catalog Number 97-66417
09 08 07   4 3 2

Global Environmental Change:
Deforestation

Deforestation is the second installment in the *Global Environmental Change Series,* which the National Science Teachers Association created in conjunction with the U.S. Environmental Protection Agency's Office of Reseach and Development. Other installments in the Series also use case studies to focus on such global environmental topics as biodiversity and population growth.

The *Global Environmental Change Series* is science based, and links the ecology and biology of global environmental changes with insights and information from other disciplines. The Series teaches students how to gather a wide range of relevant information derived from pertinent areas of study, and it encourages them to develop their own opinions in order to make decisions and solve problems.

Global Environmental Change:
Deforestation

Forests experience change, as do all of Earth's natural features. Earth's features change continually, at a variety of different rates on a variety of time scales. A continent can take eons to move meters, while a volcano or earthquake can alter thousands of hectares in a few moments. Depending on its native species, a forest can take anywhere from 200 to 500 years to reach full maturity. Such "old-growth" forests cannot be managed on a sustainable basis, requiring hundreds of years to reach climax.

While change is an integral part of Earth's natural processes, not all changes occur naturally. During the Industrial Revolution, people began realizing that the relationship between humans and Earth's natural processes was forever altered. Where ecosystems, for example, once defined and changed people, now people define and change ecosystems.

Human-induced impacts on forest ecosystems were, of course, evident even before the Industrial Revolution. Chroniclers from North Africa, the Middle East, and Europe described Rome's policy of denuding the forested lands of conquered peoples. Medieval writers recorded the retreat of forests due to growing populations among European urban centers. Present-day environmental historians analyzing pollen deposits describe how Native American peoples used fire to control forests.

The term "deforestation" became popular during the 1970s when new technologies began providing accurate means for quantifying the rates at which forests—especially tropical forests—are being cleared. As with any scientific endeavor, interpreting deforestation data is the subject of ongoing debate. Scientific estimates of global deforestation rates—and the ecological impact of those rates on Earth's natural processes—vary widely. But one thing is certain: human activity is changing the ecological role of Earth's forests at a rate faster than at any time in the last 65 million years.

What Is Deforestation?

Deforestation refers to clearing of Earth's forest cover, such as occurs when forested land is converted to cropland, pasture, human settlements, and other uses; or when a forest's trees are harvested for lumber or other wood products.

The Case Study:
Washington State's Olympic Peninsula

Since the early 17th century, the United States has lost approximately 45 percent of its old-growth forests to human-induced deforestation. One of Earth's last remaining old-growth coniferous forests stretched from Northern California to Alaska, and about 90 percent of its U.S. portion has already been cleared.

Most U.S. old-growth forests are in the Pacific Northwest, where environmental conditions support a rich diversity of life. Old-growth forests there have about twice as much biomass as any tropical forest, and contain Earth's oldest trees.

The western half of Washington State has a varied, relatively mild climate. Moist Pacific winds drop over 340 centimeters of rain along Washington State's Olympic Peninsula, where average temperatures range between 5° and 20° C, supporting both coniferous wet and dry forest ecosystems. Within Washington State's old-growth forests grow softwood trees such as Douglas fir, Sitka spruce, western hemlock, Pacific yew, and lodgepole pine. Hardwood trees include red alder, aspen, cottonwood, and maple.

Within the Olympic Peninsula, tree ages range from newly-planted to over 500 years. A few trees there are over 1,000 years old. These old-growth stands take so long to regenerate through ecological succession that they are considered non-renewable.

The Olympic Peninsula is fragmented by private, tribal, state, and federally managed holdings. Within these are late- and mid-succession ecosystems, young tree plantations, and newly planted and clear cut areas. Within the last four decades, most have been clear cut.

Western Washington State's logging industry employs more than 25,000 people, and participates in the multibillion-dollar-a-year global timber industry. While its old-growth ecosystems are biologically unique, its trees are also very valuable commercially because of their size and quality. For these and other reasons, western Washington State is at the heart of an ongoing debate about how to balance resource conservation with economic growth.

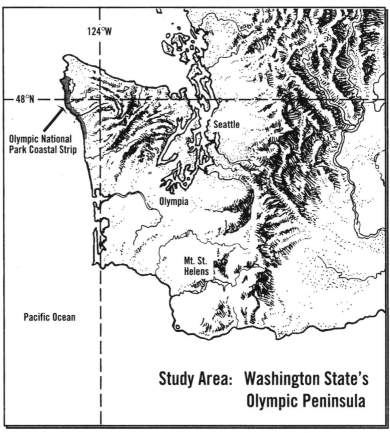

Study Area: Washington State's Olympic Peninsula

At the current rate, all unprotected old-growth forest in Washington State will be logged by 2023. Yet timber companies estimate that protecting old-growth forests will erode a major part of the region's economy. By focusing on the Olympic Peninsula as a case study, the activities in this book provide a model for addressing deforestation's ecological and economic impacts. These activities do not hand students answers, but instead provide the skills and tools to integrate science with other disciplines to gather information, make decisions, and solve problems.

5

Defining Deforestation

Background

Objective
To use maps and aerial photographs to assess change over time in a forested area.

Time Management
This activity may be completed in 1 or 2 class periods, depending on students' math skills.

Computer-aided remote sensing is one of the best tools for understanding the ecological impact of deforestation. Scientists use data compiled from aerial photographs and satellite images to view entire ecosystems in three dimensions. When analyzing a forest ecosystem, scientists feed data about biotic and abiotic components, such as species groupings and canopy heights, into a computer to generate ecologically accurate site maps. These site maps have many uses. Policy makers use them to regulate land use; land managers use them to site work areas and access roads; loggers use them to identify harvestable timber; and environmental concerns use them to monitor endangered species. We all can use these maps to better understand the impact of human activity on forest—and global—ecological processes.

Aerial photographs taken over a span of years graphically illustrate how a forest's range increases or decreases, where erosion and siltation occur, and the extent of fragmentation and "edge effects." Edge effects are generally defined as the ecological conditions that exist at ecosystem boundaries—where two or more ecosystems meet or merge. The more fragmented a forest becomes the more edges it contains. The impact of increased fragmentation and edges on an ecosystem's inhabitant species is difficult to calculate without ground studies, but aerial photographs provide scientists with a good starting point. (For a discussion of fragmentation and edge effects, see page 11.)

How much can a forest change in 10 years, and what might cause such changes? This activity uses aerial photographs of the study area—the coastal strip of Washington State's Olympic National Park on the Olympic Peninsula—to address these questions. By comparing and contrasting a 1980 aerial photograph with one from 1990, students will see how the study area changed ecologically over a 10-year period, and learn to identify some of the causes of that change.

Part A: Deriving Scale

In Part A, students derive a scale for comparing and contrasting two aerial photographs. Point out to students that several differences may occur in aerial photographs taken many years apart: the camera's altitude may be different, causing the scales to differ; the areas shown may not match up exactly; and the exposures (i.e., light and contrast) will probably be different.

Procedure

1. Divide the class into small work groups. Provide each group with photocopies of the maps and aerial photographs on pages 8 and 9.

2. Have students study the maps and photographs to familiarize themselves with the study area. If they need help, have them look at the coastline—Hoh Head, the Hoh River, and Abbey Island are easily identifiable, as are the Olympic National Park Coastal Strip's eastern boundaries and Route 101.

3. Have students derive the scales of the aerial photographs. This requires four steps for each:

a. On the road map (Figure 1), have students measure a straight line from the tip of Hoh Head to the park boundary directly to the east (about 2.25 cm). Using the scale given on the road map (0.9 cm = 1 km), have them determine the actual distance (about 2.5 km). Students may perform these same calculations using the topographic map (Figure 2), where 2.2 cm = 1 km.

b. Now have students measure the distance from the tip of Hoh Head to the park boundary on Figure 3 (approximately 4.25 cm). This measurement correlates to that of the same geographical features on the road and topographic maps. For Figure 3, 4.25 cm = 2.5 km. Students should be able to derive the scale of Figure 3 using this information (2.5/4.25 = 0.58 km, or 1 cm = 0.58 km).

c. Now have students measure Figure 3 in its entirety (11 x 17 cm^2). Students should be able to use this information to find the total area depicted in Figure 3, as in the following calculation:

$$(11 \times 0.58)(17 \times 0.58) = X \text{ km}^2$$
$$(6.38)(9.86) = X \text{ km}^2$$
$$62.9 \text{ km}^2 = X$$

Materials
Photocopies of Figures 1–4 (pages 8 and 9)
Metric rulers
Felt markers
Acetate sheets, or tracing paper

Teaching Note
U.S. Geological Survey aerial photographs and topographic maps may be obtained for a small fee. Contact:
USGS
MS804 National Center
Reston, VA 20192
USGS home page address is:
http://internet.er.usgs.gov/USGSHome.html

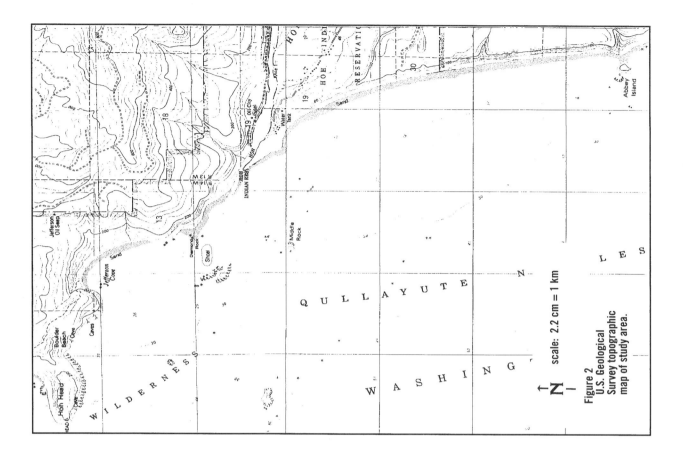

Figure 2
U.S. Geological
Survey topographic
map of study area.

scale: 2.2 cm = 1 km

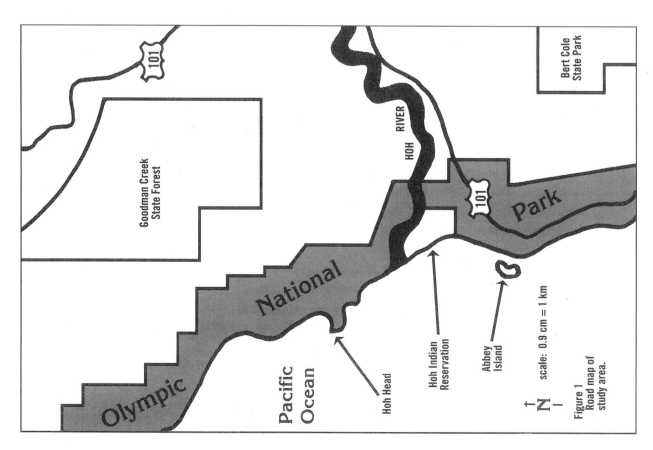

Figure 1
Road map of
study area.

scale: 0.9 cm = 1 km

Figure 4
Aerial photograph of study
area taken July 10, 1990.

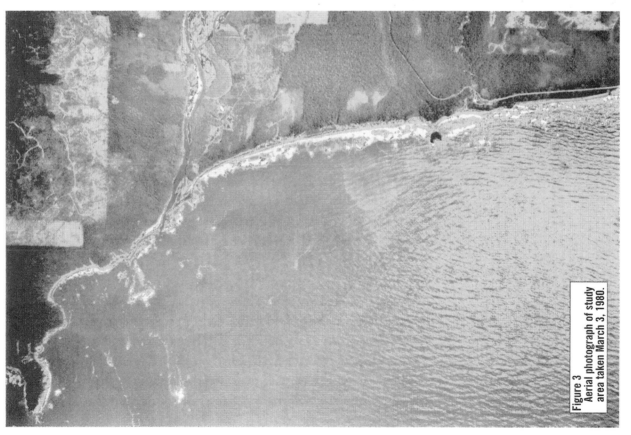

Figure 3
Aerial photograph of study
area taken March 3, 1980.

Deforestation

ACTIVITY I

Figure 3 has a total area of about 63 km². Have students calculate the total area for Figure 4.

d. To check their calculations, have students repeat these steps by measuring the distance between two other features (e.g., another point on the coast to a nearby park boundary). They should derive the same scale for Figure 3 (1 cm = 0.58 km).

Part B: Exploring Change

In Part B, students use the scales they derived in Part A to compare and contrast the two aerial photographs. As they conduct the remainder of this activity, encourage students to fully describe the environmental changes they observe on the aerial photographs.

Procedure

1. Once students have derived the scale of the aerial photographs, have them use their rulers and an acetate sheet or tracing paper to make a reference grid for studying environmental change. Each of the grid's squares should measure 1 cm² and be numbered for reference.

2. Turn student attention to Figure 3, the 1980 aerial photograph. Have them place the reference grid on Figure 3 and identify several places where logging has occurred. Have them mark these locations on the grid.

3. Now turn student attention to Figure 4, the 1990 aerial photograph. Have them describe, either orally or in writing, the changes they observe over this 10-year period.

4. Have students calculate the total area logged between 1980 and 1990 for the areas south and east of Hoh Head. To do this, have them lay a reference grid on the 1980 aerial photograph, trace the logged areas, and color them in. (For reference as to placement, also have them trace the coastline.)

5. Now have students lay the same reference grid on the 1990 aerial photograph, adjusting it to make sure the geographic features are aligned as closely as possible. Have students trace the newly logged areas, measure them, and calculate their areas. Once students have completed these steps, have them add their totals together. The result is a reasonably close estimate of the total area of the study site harvested between 1980 and 1990.

Figure 5

As students work with the aerial photographs in this activity, encourage them to observe the patchwork quality of the landscapes they depict. In the Olympic Peninsula, this is the result of a variety of factors, especially timber harvesting practices and government land-use regulations. Such human activities are serving to create extensive edge ecosystems, which are in turn having a profound effect on the responses of biological species in terms of their ability to meet nutritional and habitat needs. So great is the impact of human activity on existing ecosystems that edge ecology has become a sub-discipline in its own right.

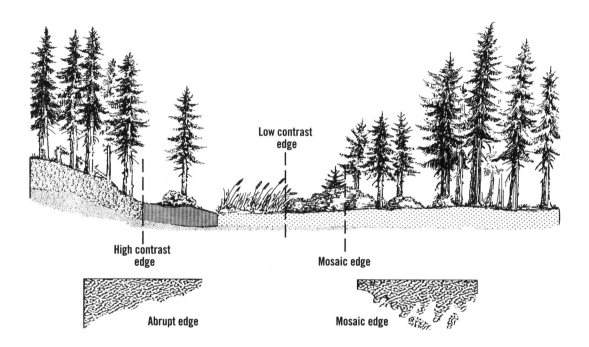

Low contrast edge

High contrast edge

Mosaic edge

Abrupt edge

Mosaic edge

What are fragmentation and edge effects?

Many animal species require extended areas of continuous, uninterrupted habitat to meet their biological needs, such as hunting for food and nurturing their young. All of Earth's ecosystems—from tropical rain forests to dry scrub tundras—contain such species. When human activity diminishes an ecosystem's range or dramatically alters its configuration, the most profoundly affected species are those with such needs.

An ecosystem is called *fragmented* when it ceases to be a continuous range of uninterrupted habitat and assumes a patchwork quality. The patchwork quality of the Olympic Peninsula's forest ecosystem is readily noticeable in this activity's aerial photographs. As its forested areas have become further and further diminished, the Peninsula's ecosystem has become less and less capable of meeting the basic biological needs of many of its inhabitant species. (For a discussion of deforestation's affect on a species indigenous to the Olympic Peninsula, see page 38.)

Deforestation causes increased fragmentation, which increases the number of edges in a forest ecosystem. In ecology, an *edge* is where two or more different vegetational communities meet. (This should not be confused with an *ecotone*, which is where two or more vegetational communities not only meet but merge.) Some edges result from natural conditions, such as distinctive changes in soil type, topographical differences, geomorphic differences (e.g., rock outcroppings), and micro-climatic changes. Other edges result from natural disturbances, such as fires, storms, and floods. But more and more edges are the result of human activity, especially development, livestock grazing, agriculture, and deforestation.

Flora species found among fragmented forest edges tend to be opportunistic and shade tolerant, while fauna species found there usually require two or more vegetational communities for their survival and reproduction. Unless forest species faced with increased fragmentation and edge habitats can adapt—which means finding new ways to meet basic biological needs—they must either emigrate or perish.

There is a limit to how small an ecosystem can become and still support the biological needs of many species. Over time, an ecosystem can become so diminished, fragmented, and edge-filled that it becomes dominated by edge species.

Questions for Discussion

1. Ask students to consider why the Olympic National Park Coastal Strip's boundary is so clearly identifiable in Figure 3.

2. Logging is not allowed in national parks, but is allowed in national forests. For each of the aerial photographs, have students differentiate between undisturbed forest, newly cut forest, and harvested areas where new growth is occurring. Encourage them to define the evidence on which they base their differentiations.

3. Ask students to comment on what has happened to the land east of Hoh Head. Invite them to provide explanations for what has happened to this relatively barren area.

4. Have students look at the areas immediately adjacent to the Olympic National Park Coastal Strip. Ask them if there were significant changes in continuous forest among those areas between 1980 and 1990.

5. For step 4, have students estimate the total percentage of the area logged between 1980 and 1990. Ask them if this total is equal to the total amount of habitat loss for the animal species that inhabit this area of the Olympic Peninsula's forest ecosystem.

6. Have students look at the two aerial photographs, and ask them which contains more dark areas. Can they identify reasons why one should contain more dark areas than the other?

7. Have students look at the topographic map and make general assessments about the geography of the areas outside the park which have not been logged. Ask them what factors might act as a control on logging in areas close to roads where the land is relatively accessible.

8. Ask students how long they think it takes a forest to grow back for future harvest. Remind them that climate conditions and tree species type help determine how fast a forest regenerates.

Answers to Discussion Questions

1. The park boundary is clearly identifiable because it is the only area that has not been logged at all in recent years.

2. Undisturbed, continuous forest appears darkest on both photographs. Newly cut areas appear lightest, and harvested areas where growth is occurring appear light grey.

3. It has been logged, possibly clear cut.

4. Yes, there were significant changes.

5. A workable estimate is approximately 50 percent. No, the actual amount of habitat loss is probably greater than the total area of forest logged because of the impact of fragmentation and edge effects on inhabitant animal species. See page 11, "What are fragmentation and edge effects?," for a discussion of how habitat reduction and fragmentation affect animal species.

6. The 1980 aerial photograph should appear darker than the 1990 aerial photograph. Several factors taken together probably account for this, such as differences in weather conditions, different camera altitudes, and different camera exposures. (The photocopying process required for this activity may also account for some variations in contrast.) However, students should be encouraged to observe that the 1990 aerial photograph shows less overall forested area. Because forest vegetation appears darkest of all the vegetational communities shown in each photograph, and the 1990 photograph shows less overall forested area than the 1980 photograph, the 1980 photograph appears darker than the 1990 photograph.

7. Their assessment should include factors that can either help or hinder logging, such as elevation, the existence of rivers or roads, and legal restrictions on logging old-growth areas.

8. A workable average time from seedling to harvestable size for most commercially grown tree species is 20–40 years. The discussion on page 14, "How are forests managed and harvested?," provides further elaboration on this question.

How are forests managed and harvested?

Forestry is the practice of managing and harvesting timber for human use. By treating trees just like any other agricultural crop, its goal is to provide a continual supply of wood products, such as lumber, paper, and charcoal. To achieve this, foresters balance their annual harvest with the rate of tree growth. This balance is called *sustained yield*. To achieve sustained yield, foresters try to ensure that they have trees of equal yield—of similar ages and sizes—from seedlings to mature trees.

In the Pacific Northwest, forests are harvested 20 to 40 years after planting. The length of this cycle depends on how fast the particular tree species grows and the desired size and quality of the wood. Old-growth forests cannot be managed on a sustainable basis—true old growth requires hundreds of years. That is why there is so much debate about old-growth logging. Once cut, old-growth trees cannot be replaced within human lifetimes.

Logging companies use several different methods to harvest trees. *Clear cutting* is the removal of every tree in a designated area regardless of tree size. It is used to remove a mature stand of trees, and to replace an existing stand with one that is more uniform in age and size. Some species, such as Douglas fir, will not grow in shade and can best be replanted only in clear cut areas. From a commercial perspective, clear cutting is the most efficient logging method. But from an ecological perspective, it greatly diminishes an area's biological diversity by removing habitat. It also removes nutrients that would have found their way back into soils through decomposition. Depending upon an area's geology and topography, clear cutting can accelerate soil erosion. Soil-laden runoff diminishes water quality.

Seed tree cutting clear cuts an area, but leaves a few trees standing in order to reseed it. After the seed trees have established a new stand, they are also cut. Seed tree cutting is used with loblolly and other southern pines. Seed tree cutting allows some natural regeneration of an area. Its environmental impacts are similar to those of clear cutting.

In *shelterwood cutting*, logging companies harvest a stand of timber in several stages over 10 to 20 years, establishing new trees as older ones are harvested. Shelterwood cutting leaves some older trees to provide shade for seedlings. It is best suited for trees such as oak and white pine, which grow best in shade during their first few years. Shelterwood cutting results in a forest that is more diverse in age than a forest which has been clear cut and replanted. It also may result in less erosion. Shelterwood cutting may result in a smaller yield of trees at any one harvest than clear cuts, but it does provide a steady supply.

Logging companies use *selection cutting* to harvest mature trees in order to make room for younger ones. Some large trees are left to produce seeds. Stands that have been selectively cut retain most of their canopy, and so work well with tree species that prefer shade in their early growth. Selection cutting is more labor intensive and costly than clear cutting, but may result in less ecological damage. Forests are harvested through selection cutting every five to 30 years, depending on their tree species. Selection cutting retains more of a forest's biological diversity than do other harvesting techniques.

Figures 6 and 7
These two photographs show the area around the main building at Western Washington State University.
Figure 6 shows the area immediately after it was clear cut in 1899; Figure 7 shows the same area in 1995.

Suggestions for Further Study

• If there is managed timber in your county or region, have students investigate what tree species grow there. What kind of harvesting techniques work best for the different tree species they identify? What criteria are they using to determine what the "best" method is? Students may wish to research and discuss the various harvesting techniques they identify.

• Managed timber may be found growing on both public and private lands. Your county extension agent can provide assistance as to the commercial value of managed timber in your area, and describe the forest management techniques used by various logging concerns. Contact the U.S. Department of Agriculture, of which the U.S. Forest Service is a part, and the U.S. Department of the Interior, of which the U.S. National Park Service is a part, to obtain public information about tree growing and harvesting. The Resources List beginning on page 58 provides contact addresses, phone numbers, and websites for these and other government agencies.

• Logging companies will also provide information about forest management and logging practices. Companies such as Georgia Pacific and Weyerhauser may be contacted by looking up their local representatives in the telephone book. Students may wish to write them requesting information about their timber management and harvesting techniques, or invite a representative to speak in the classroom. Check the Resources List for contact information.

• The history of the United States Government's environmental policy—especially regarding forest and water resources—is distinctly tied to questions about balancing resource conservation with economic growth. The U.S. Forest Service, created in 1902 by President Theodore Roosevelt, was originally charged with identifying lands to be brought into the public domain and managing them using sustained yield techniques. Students may be interested to learn that the Progressive Era—roughly 1895 to 1915—saw as much debate, discussion, and contention over national environmental policy questions as they see in today's news and on television. Have them compare the questions people were asking then with the questions people are asking now about resource conservation and economic growth. A good starting point is to conduct research on Gifford Pinchot, the first U.S. Forest Service Chief. The Gifford Pinchot National Historic Site is located in Milford, Pennsylvania, and contains many archival holdings pertaining to the origins and evolution of U.S. environmental policy.

Ecological Succession

Background

Objective
To understand how a forest changes ecologically during its stages of succession.

Time Management
This activity can be completed in 1 class period. Photocopies may be distributed to individuals or groups of students, depending on your classroom organization.

Forest ecosystems are often disturbed by fires, landslides, and human activity, such as clear cutting. But do such disturbances mean the end of a forest ecosystem? No because, through succession, a forest regenerates by changing over time from a youthful, fast-growing ecosystem to a mature, slow-growing or climax ecosystem. The various stages of succession are orderly and predictable. However, one ecological community of species may take decades or even centuries to completely succeed another ecological community of species.

This activity enables students to explore several stages of succession in a forest ecosystem over time by taking a "field trip." The field trip begins by "visiting" a site in Washington State's Olympic Peninsula, observing how it looks now, then inferring what it may have looked like in the past and what it might look like in the future. By studying four stages of succession, students will understand the natural forces by which one ecological community of species succeeds another. They will also learn to scientifically explain patterns of growth during an ecosystem's maturation process.

This field trip visits a site in the lowland forests of the Pacific Northwest, in a coastal area at an elevation of about 180 meters. (Some Pacific Northwest forests grow at heights of more than 920 meters.) The site stays the same, but students visit it at critical stages in its 300-year development from disturbance to maturity.

Why is red alder a pioneer species?

Forested land quickly loses its soluble nutrients and minerals after disturbances such as clear cutting, landslides, and soil erosion. Nitrogen is one of the most important nutrients for forest regeneration, and red alders play a significant role in restoring nitrogen back into the soil after a disturbance.

Trees need nitrogen to grow, but most species can neither generate their own nitrogen nor obtain it from the air. They must rely on nitrogen compounds in soils. Red alders, however, are able to obtain nitrogen directly from the air. The inset to Site II (page 19) shows nodules covering the surfaces of a red alder's root system. The nodules contain nitrogen-fixing bacteria that convert atmospheric nitrogen into a chemical form usable by plants. When the red alder decomposes, this usable nitrogen is added to the soil's nutrient supply and becomes available to successive plant species.

Procedure

Site I

1. Have students examine Site I. Encourage them to describe how the forest ecosystem has been disturbed. Have students describe, either orally or in writing, the probable fate of the ecosystem's organisms, and what they think might happen to the soil.

Site II

2. Have students examine Site II. If Site I experiences no human intervention, this is what it would look like about 15 years later. The dominant tree species is red alder, but grass makes up much of the ground cover. Several other plant species grow in spaces between the grass and red alders, attracting deer and other grazers. Encourage students to notice the young evergreens beneath the red alders. These are Douglas firs, and cannot grow in soil lacking nitrogen.

Site III

3. Have students examine Site III. It depicts Site I without human intervention 60–75 years later. Encourage students to observe that red alders and grasses have now been replaced by Douglas firs and broad-leaf maples, and the floor is covered with sword ferns as well as some younger Douglas firs. Two new tree species have appeared in the understory: western red cedar and western hemlock.

Site IV

4. Have students examine Site IV, which depicts Site I without human intervention 270–300 years later. The dominant tree species are western red cedar and western hemlock. Sword ferns dominate the forest floor. There are no large Douglas firs, having been out-competed by the more opportunistic and shade-tolerant cedars and hemlocks.

Encourage students to notice that the young trees in the understory are western red cedars and western hemlocks. No young Douglas firs are to be seen competing for light in the darkened forest. Thick black loam makes up the forest soil. On the soil's surface are the decomposing parts of fallen trees, as well as scattered pieces of lichens and mosses which contain nitrogen compounds made in the canopy. Even in the dry heat of late summer, the ground remains moist and the air stays cool.

The forest ecosystem depicted in Site IV has reached its climax stage of succession. The plant community is described as a western red cedar/western hemlock climax forest. The forest is mature and ecologically stable. If the climate stays the same, the forest will remain unchanged indefinitely—or at least until the next disturbance.

Materials
Photocopies of:
Site I   (page 18)
Site II   (page 19)
Site III   (page 20)
Site IV   (page 21)

17

Teaching Note
If you show students photocopies of the four sites one at a time, have them form hypotheses about what each site might look like about 15 or 30 years later.

Site I

ACTIVITY 2

18

Red alder

Young red alder

Young Douglas fir

Nitrogen-fixing root nodules

Deforestation

Site III

Broadleaf maple

Douglas fir

Young red cedar

Young Douglas fir

Young western hemlock

Sword ferns

Site IV

Western red cedar

Western hemlock

Young western hemlock

Sword ferns

Deforestation

ACTIVITY 2

Questions for Discussion

Site I

1. What will happen to the exposed soil on the site?

2. What will happen to mineral nutrients that were in the forest soil before the disturbance?

Site II

1. In the absence of red alders, what plants might grow first on Site II if nutrients were abundant, or if humans added nitrogen to the soil?

Site III

1. Ask students what they think killed off the red alders and grasses that were living on Site II.

2. Ask students how they think the Douglas firs and broadleaf maples get their nitrogen now that the nitrogen-fixing alders are gone. (Hint: The Douglas firs' bark, especially on the crown, is covered with lichens and mosses.)

3. How does the soil at Site III compare with the soil at Site II?

4. How did the seeds of western red cedars and western hemlocks come to be at Site III?

Site IV

1. Invite students to consider what ways light and nutrients determine the course of succession.

2. Have students discuss what factors play a role in influencing succession in the forests of the Pacific Northwest.

How does succession affect energy flow?

The relationship between energy flow and succession is based on a concept presented by ecologist Howard Odum in 1969. Odum's thesis was that succession involves a fundamental shift in energy flow. As a forest succeeds towards climax, increased amounts of energy are relegated to biomass maintenance rather than to production. Thus, in the climax ecosystem, maximum biomass is supported per unit of energy flow. Since biomass represents stored energy, power output is maximized in the climax ecosystem. Figure 5 shows how production, biomass, and respiration shift over time in a generalized successional forest ecosystem.

To help students understand how energy flow and succession inform timber harvesting practices, have them assume they are forest managers. Tell them they must harvest their forest's trees at just the right time to yield the greatest amount of timber while requiring the least amount of human effort. Have them use the energy flow and succession information in Figure 5 to determine the best time to harvest.

Why is this an important question for forest managers? Forest managers want to harvest as much biomass as possible, so they want to target a time immediately after the greatest production of plant tissue when respiration has begun to decline. The trees will have had their growth spurt and will be beginning to settle into old-growth maturity.

Thus, for the generalized successional forest ecosystem represented in Figure 5, students should target a period between 60–90 years to harvest. To cut earlier, the forester wouldn't benefit from the growth spurt; to cut later wouldn't provide much more timber.

How does a grassy area, such as that shown in Site II, compare with the old-growth climax forest, such as that depicted in Site IV more than 150 years later? As students use Figure 5 to formulate their answers, have them consider the roles of the following factors:

light	wind
temperature	water vapor pressure
water budget	soil accumulation
water in soil	soil development
soil organic matter	soil minerals

A typical, human-managed grassy area (i.e., a lawn) is an arrested, fast-growing ecosystem at the successional level of Site II. Gross productivity and respiration are high, accumulated biomass is low. Much of the solar energy entering the system is lost to reflection. The lawn is fragile, requiring continuous watering, regular fertilizing, mowing, treatment for disease, and the "shooing" of such grazers as deer and moles.

The old-growth climax forest is a slow-growing mature ecosystem at the successional stage of Site IV. Production and respiration are low, accumulated biomass is high and of good quality. Only a little energy escapes from the forest. Even the temperatures are relatively cool and steady.

23

Figure 5
As energy flows through a forest ecosystem, some of it gets used to produce new plant tissue through photosynthesis and some of it gets used to maintain the organisms' physiological functions. For example, a forest's annual gross productivity might be a million tons of plant tissue while its normal respiration might be 200,000 metric tons, making its net productivity 800,000 metric tons. The stylized graph below depicts the relationship in a generalized successional forest ecosystem between tissue production (Gross Productivity), system maintenance (Respiration), and tissue accumulation (Biomass) over a 300-year period. The Y axis measures energy conversion, usually in metric tons.

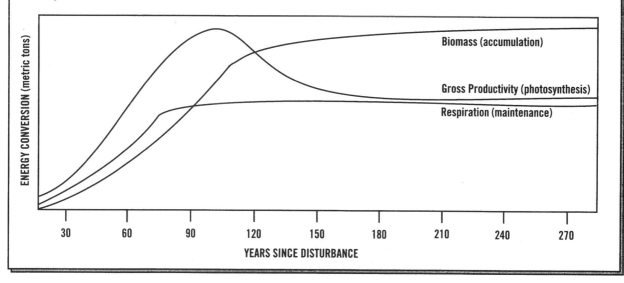

Answers to Discussion Questions

Site I

1. Exposed soil will wash away, filling creeks, rivers, lakes, and bays with silt. New plant communities cannot reestablish themselves easily in areas where the land has been depleted of soil and soil nutrients.

2. Nutrients dissolve in rainwater and are carried away by the runoff.

Site II

1. Given a soil fertilized with nitrogen, Douglas firs and broadleaf maples could immediately establish themselves on the disturbed land. (Note: Foresters practice this type of intervention before planting replacement trees soon after a harvest.)

Site III

1. The red alders at Site II are killed off by the shade of over-growing Douglas firs and broadleaf maples.

2. Mosses and lichens grow all over the trees, expecially on branches exposed to the sun. Pieces of moss, lichen, and fern fall to the ground and decay, thus enriching the soil with nitrogen they fixed from the air.

3. Soil in a climax forest is loamier, or richer, due to many years of organic accumulation.

4. Seeds of western red cedars and hemlocks are food for birds and mammals. Those seeds that are carried away, dropped by animals, or blown in by winds will germinate and grow in the rich soil at Site III.

Site IV

1. The trees of the forest compete for sun and nutrient minerals. At first, alders capture the sun while other trees fail to grow for lack of essential minerals. Later, Douglas firs and broadleaf maples shade out the alders after they have enriched the soil. Still later, the highly shade-tolerant western red cedars and hemlocks shade out all other species.

2. Light and mineral nutrients continue to influence succession at high elevations. In addition, low temperatures and heavy winter snows influence the course of succession on Pacific Northwest mountains.

Suggestions for Further Study

• Succession occurs for all forests and other ecosystems throughout the world. Have students describe succession in their own region's various ecosystems.

• Have students research the growth requirements of the lodgepole pine, which requires the intense heat from fire to reproduce. Have them compare and contrast the "prevent all fires" and "let it burn" theories of forest management.

• Ask students to research Surtsey, a volcanic island that formed off southern Iceland in 1963. Because it was an entirely new land formation completely isolated by water, Surtsey presented a rare chance for scientists to study how life colonizes a large, newly formed area. Have students report their findings, either orally or in writing, and compare them with what they learned in this activity. For example, there are no forests in the Icelandic ecosystem so, after mosses and weather break the lava down into soil, grasses define the ecosystem's climax vegetational community.

• Have students research the succession of bog ecosystems found at higher latitudes. Invite them to consider what factors drive the ecosystem's ecological change from standing water to peat moss to spruce forest.

• Programs that plant new trees after older trees have been harvested or cut down are called reforestation programs. Logging companies often want to reforest an area by planting only one species of tree because that will maximize their profits. Have students consider how such practices might affect the ecology of a forest ecosystem.

Soil Erosion

Objective
To analyze natural agents of erosion and factors that control erosion.

Background

In this activity, students conduct at least three rounds of erosion trials to observe various causes and control mechanisms. They develop an understanding of how deforested land is especially vulnerable to erosion and why this can be a problem. As students use the stream table models to explore how erosion is caused and controlled, their appreciation of a systematic approach to scientific experimentation is reinforced.

Given enough time, an inactive Earth would be reduced to almost featureless, level continents with sluggish rivers wandering across their surfaces. But Earth is not inactive. Mountain-building processes, driven by Earth's internal heat and other forces, create elevated areas—which wind and water, driven by solar energy and gravity, sculpt into landscapes. Dramatic examples of these processes include the Grand Canyon, the Andes, the Mariana Trench, and the Himalayas.

Erosion is an important part of the natural process of mountain building and destruction. Erosion is the reduction of Earth's surface by removal of materials. Agents of erosion include wind, water, ice, and time. Forests slow erosion with their extensive root systems, which help hold soil in place. In old-growth and climax forests, a thick canopy also keeps heavy rains from slowly chipping away at the land.

Human intervention in Earth's natural processes can alter erosion rates. In the cases of unregulated logging, development, and poor farming practices, human influences may lead to a significant erosion of land and increased river sedimentation. On the other hand, human influences can also slow erosion rates. One method of erosion control is placing heavy material in a stream channel to hinder water flow. The material, often composed of stones, boulders, cement slabs, and other materials, is referred to as rip-rap.

Time Management
This activity may be completed in 1–2 class periods. Steps 1–8 can be completed during the first session, and steps 9–13 during the second.

Figure 1
Erosion is a natural process. Pictured here is Dry Falls, Washington State, the site of a 400-foot-high waterfall during the Pleistocene Era's "Spokane floods." This site may once have been covered by as much as 200 feet of water.

Procedure

1. Simple stream tables can be constructed from pop flats (the cardboard boxes that cases of soda are sold in) or any low cardboard box, by lining them with 2 mil plastic sheeting. For more elaborate stream tables, ask your industrial arts teacher to construct them from plywood and lumber, then line them with the plastic sheeting. Figure 2 depicts a simple stream table.

Materials
Stream tables, or shallow cardboard boxes like those containing four six-packs
Plastic sheeting, 2 mil thick
Assorted wood blocks
Soil and sand samples
Sod squares
Water
Small sticks and pebbles
Paper towels
Sketch paper and pencils
Student Observation Sheets (page 33)

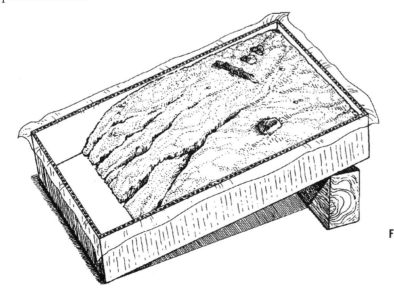

Figure 2
A simple stream table using a shallow, cardboard flat lined with 2 mil-thick plastic sheeting.

Class Organization
Groups may work together to run parallel tests of variables, depending on the number of groups and the amount of time available. For instance, two groups may want to test elevation, so one group can elevate its stream table 5 cm and the other 10 cm. Both groups should use the same volumes of water poured at the same rates onto the same soil types.

Teaching Note
The amount of soil and sand needed for this activity depends on how many students are in your class, and on both the size and number of stream tables you have them use. Conduct a test run with a single table before deciding how much is enough for the entire class.

2. Lead a pre-activity discussion to discover students' perceptions of erosion. Ask if they have ever seen evidence of erosion, and have them describe what they saw. Have them develop a list of causes and controls of erosion based on this discussion. Do not comment on their perceptions at this time, but have a volunteer write the class' list on the board.

3. Divide the class into groups of three or four students. If possible, let each group choose which soil or sand mixtures they will use in their stream table. Some students may want to work with top soil, some with sand, and some with a mixture of soil and sand. Students may wish to bring soil and sand from home.

4. Provide each group with soil or sand, a stream table, and a water source. Do not give them the organic or "rip-rap" material (i.e., small sticks and pebbles) at this time.

5. Have students place their soil or sand in the stream table and tamp it down. Soil or sand should be arranged to cover about 3/4 of the table bottom leaving the other 1/4 bare, as shown in Figure 3. After students elevate the soil end of their stream tables, have them record the elevation height on their Student Observation Sheets.

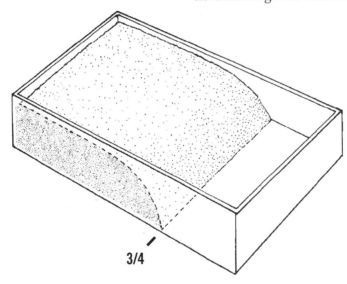

3/4

Figure 3
Arrange the soil in the stream table so it covers about 3/4 of the table's surface and leaves the remaining 1/4 bare, as depicted at left. You may want to cut a drainage hole in the bare area to allow excess water to escape.

6. As a first trial, have one student per group sprinkle water on the soil or sand. Have students conduct further trials using different variables, such as the quantity of water poured, the rate at which it is poured (i.e., slow, medium, or fast), and the distance between the water source and the soil or sand surface. Have students keep accurate records of the conditions of each trial on a Student Observation Sheet. Have them sketch their observations before and after each trial.

7. After students become comfortable working with their stream tables, stop the activity and have them describe what they saw. Their Student Observation Sheets will help them distinguish among the trials they have conducted and focus their ideas on the erosion they observed.

8. Have the groups compare how their stream tables were alike and how they differed. Have the class discuss some of the variables they observed, and how changing one or more might affect erosion rates. Variables for them to consider might include: soil type and density, water volume, how fast the water is sprinkled on, stream table slope, and how firmly the soil is packed.

9. Ask students how they think they might control or diminish the erosion they observed. Write their suggestions on the board.

Teaching Note
If class time is running short, break the activity between steps 8 and 9.

10. Based on their discussion from steps 8 and 9, have each group choose a variable, alter it, and conduct new trials. Provide new Student Observation Sheets. Have students describe why they chose that particular variable. Is it because they think it might serve to control erosion? If so, how has the erosion process differed from the first to the second round of trials? Have students refer to their previous Student Observation Sheets for comparison.

11. Now provide each group with rip-rap materials, such as small sticks and pebbles. Have them conduct new erosion trials, using new Student Observation Sheets to maintain accurate records. Students may wish to develop their own erosion control methods using materials found in the classroom or brought from home.

12. Have students replace the soil or sand in their stream tables with sod squares. (They may have to gently shake each square in order to remove some soil so the squares will fit in their stream tables.) Provide new Student Observation Sheets, and have the groups conduct a third round of trials, first with and then without erosion controls. Make sure they use their Student Observation Sheets to keep accurate records.

Teaching Note
To prepare the sod samples for placement, first cut the squares to fit in the stream table and then clip the grass as short as possible.

13. Conduct a general class discussion to allow students to compare and contrast erosion rates among the various trials they've conducted. Encourage them to refer to the appropriate Student Observation Sheet so they may accurately describe specific points of interest during this discussion. You may wish to take this opportunity to point out the value of compiling and maintaining accurate data in any scientific undertaking.

Questions for Discussion

1. In steps 10-12, students tried various erosion control methods. Ask them to describe the results of their attempts. What worked? What didn't? How could the stream table be improved to better model causes of erosion and erosion control mechanisms?

2. Ask students why they think flash flooding is more likely to happen after several days of continual rain.

3. Mountain trails, especially up steep inclines, are cut diagonally up the mountain, as shown in Figure 4. In the Grand Canyon, for example, mules travel a roundabout path to arrive at the base of the canyon. This same type of "switchback" is used to control erosion in forested areas. Ask students why hikers in mountains are asked to stay on marked trails, and not cut through the woods even though their hike would be shorter.

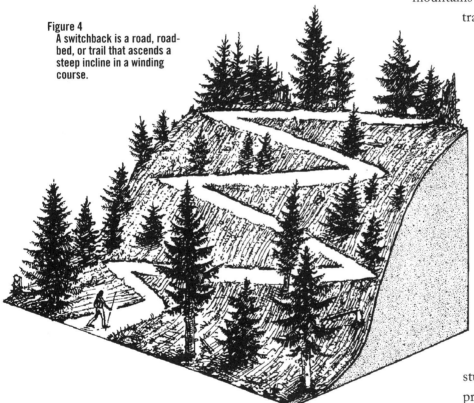

Figure 4
A switchback is a road, roadbed, or trail that ascends a steep incline in a winding course.

4. Logging roads and back country areas are often closed to four-wheel-drive vehicles and mountain bicycles. Lead students in a discussion about why these roads might be closed. Can they relate their own observations from their stream table models to the discussion?

5. Logging roads often have shallow ditches cut across them at regular intervals. Ask students why they think this practice helps control erosion.

6. Discuss with students how time, slope, and the rate and amount of water affect the amount of erosion that occurs.

7. Ask students why they think clear cut areas in forests or bare farm land are more susceptible to erosion than are undisturbed areas.

Answers to Discussion Questions

1. When rip-rap is added to the channels, it changes the direction of flow and, in most cases, slows down the flow. Unless properly placed, the rip-rap will in some cases increase the rate of erosion as the water is diverted into a different channel or the flow is constricted. If allowed to run long enough, the water will wash away the rip-rap rendering it ineffective.

2. The ground will be saturated, which will allow little infiltration to take place and the water will run off.

3. The main reason is that hiking trails are often laid out so they may take advantage of the topography to control runoff. By cutting through the forest, the hiker will inadvertently create a new, steeper trail that could disturb the surface and increase erosion.

4. Ruts from tires create natural channels that force the water into a narrow stream instead of letting it spread out and infiltrate.

5. The ditches stop the water from flowing down the road and divert it to the side. The water is thus kept from gaining too much speed and collecting sediment. This slows the effect of erosion.

6. Student answers will vary, but should center on rate of erosion and amount of materials moved.

7. Student answers will vary, but should focus on how disturbed surfaces erode faster. Students should be encouraged to refer to their Student Observation Sheets to address this question.

Vocabulary

Erosion: Reduction of Earth's surface by removal or redistribution of materials.

Ground cover: Any type of vegetation that protects against runoff.

Infiltration: Movement of water into Earth.

Mass wastage: Any downslope movement of Earth materials.

Meandering: The movement of a stream channel into broad sweeping curves.

Runoff: Movement of water over Earth's surface.

Weathering: Chemical and mechanical processes that reduce rock to sediments.

Loam: Soil that is 7–27 percent clay, 28–50 percent silt, and up to 52 percent sand.

Suggestions for Further Study

• Have each group model a single effect of erosion. They should develop the project themselves—from choosing the effect to deciding which materials they need to demonstrate it. Have them build the models and demonstrate them to the class. Encourage the groups to relate their models to actual erosion.

• Soils exist in a variety of types. Have students use soil reference books to write a report on the origins of different soils and how soil scientists classify them.

• Either as a class trip or as a project for each group, have students visit some construction sites. Have them observe the erosion control methods they encounter and evaluate their effectiveness.

What is the ecological importance of forests?

Forest ecosystems, such as the old-growth forest ecosystem in this case study, provide habitats for more species of flora and fauna than any other of Earth's ecosystems. This means that forests are Earth's primary biodiversity reservoirs.

Forests also serve as giant sponges, acting as an impediment to runoff by absorbing and holding onto water. In this way, forests regulate the flow of water from mountainous to more low–lying areas, play an important role in controlling soil erosion, and reduce the amounts of sedimentation that wash into bodies of water such as rivers, lakes, and estuaries.

Mature forest ecosystems, such as old-growth forests, are a key component in global biogeochemical cycling. Here are some of the ways forests contribute to the carbon, nitrogen, and phosphorous cycles:

• Carbon—terrestrial primary producers absorb atmospheric carbon dioxide and convert it into complex carbohydrates through photosynthesis. Aerobic respiration in oxygen-consuming producers and consumers converts glucose and other complex compounds back into carbon dioxide. Mature forest ecosystems are one of the principal terrestrial links in the circulation of carbon in the biosphere.

• Nitrogen—organisms require nitrogen to make proteins, DNA, RNA, and other organic compounds. But the nitrogen gas in the troposphere can't be used directly by multi-celled organisms. Converting atmospheric nitrogen into chemical forms useful to plants is performed mostly by cyanobacteria in soils and water, as well as by *Rhizobium* bacteria that live in nodules attached to root systems of some plants (see page 16). Cyanobacteria convert nitrogen into water-soluble ionic compounds that are then absorbed through those root systems and made available to consumer organisms.

• Phosphorous—released by the slow weathering of rock deposits, phosphorous is dissolved in soil water and absorbed through plant root systems. Consumers get their phosphorous by eating producers or animals that have eaten producers. Animal waste and decay materials return much of this phosphorous to soils and water bodies.

In most forest ecosystems, a significant percentage of the overall nutrient pool—especially nitrogen, phosphorous, and sulfur—is found in soils. A forest's extensive root system combines with piled-up debris and decaying underbrush to prevent soil erosion, thus preventing nutrient removal. Because of these and other ecological contributions, the ecological value of a typical tree has been estimated at almost $200,000 worth of oxygen production, air and water cleansing, habitat provision, soil fertility, erosion control, and many other benefits. The same tree sold as timber on the commercial market might fetch about $600.

Student Observation Sheet

Group Name: _____   Trial Number: _____

Trial Conditions

soil type used _____

elevation of stream table _____

amount of water poured on _____

height water poured from _____

other factors _____

_____

_____

_____

Sketch Area

before	after

Questions

1. When you first added water, did it begin to run off immediately? Describe what you saw. Why do you think the water behaved as it did?

2. As the water moved across the surface it probably formed channels in the soil. Describe the process of channelization. How did the water affect the channel?

3. Compare your observations with groups that used other materials. What do you think might account for any similarities and differences in your results?

ACTIVITY 3

Deforestation

Habitat Loss and Inhabitant Species

Background

Objective
To develop scientific tools for analyzing the ecological conditions of a habitat.

Figure 1
The northern spotted owl, *Strix occidentalis caurina*, is territorial and lives primarily in 200-year-old Douglas firs in the Pacific Northwest. Each nesting pair requires 900–1,800 hectares of old-growth forest to meet its habitat requirements.

Deforestation affects all the species that inhabit a forest ecosystem, both flora and fauna. Many animal species rely on a forest to support their biological needs. When deforestation changes a forest's ecological conditions it can become significantly less able to support those needs.

An ecosystem's ability to provide a suitable habitat for a species is defined ecologically by a combination of abiotic and biotic factors, including temperature, rainfall, humidity, soil type, wind speed and direction, sunlight, and vegetation characteristics such as density. Suitable habitat for any species is that which supports a stable or increasing population. When scientists develop and evaluate an environmental management plan or impact statement, they first compile data about the type, quality, and amount of suitable habitat the environment contains. In this activity, students first work with the same tools scientists use to compile data about habitat suitability, and then explore the impact of habitat loss on inhabitant species.

In Part A, students analyze a familiar, local habitat and, working with habitat analysis tools, develop an understanding of the link between a habitat's ecological characteristics and the biological needs of its inhabitants. In Part B, students analyze how habitat loss has affected a particular species, one indigenous to Pacific Northwest old-growth forests, the northern spotted owl (Figure 1).

Part A: Analyzing Habitat

In Part A, students analyze the ecological conditions of a habitat with which they are familiar. Students quantify the site's abiotic components and catalog its inhabitant species. As they do so, have students consider the overall ecological impact of even slight variations in the site's ecological conditions.

Procedure

Time Management
Parts A and B of this activity can be completed in 1 class period each.

Materials
Thermometers
Wind sock or vane
Colored pencils
Tape measure
Wooden stakes (at least four)

1. Select a local site for study. A good site will include several ecosystem components, such as a grassy area and a wooded area. Use a tape measure to survey 30 m², and mark off the corners with the stakes.

2. Select and mark off key areas in which to take measurements. Select a few different areas for taking measurements, such as under a tree, in some tall grass, in a mowed area, on a sidewalk, and so forth.

3. Have students make a list of the ecological conditions they want to examine. Their list should include abiotic characteristics—such as temperature, humidity, rainfall, wind speed and direction, sunlight, and soil type—and biotic characteristics, such as what vegetation species are present and in what densities.

4. Arrange students into groups (three per group works well for making these types of measurements). Divide the groups into those who will study habitat and those who will study species.

5. Have the habitat groups rotate around the different areas to take and record measurements. Note: Groups should visit each site several times so they can average the data together.

Measuring ecological conditions

Scientists use a variety of resources and tools to compile data about an ecosystem's ecological conditions. Depending on the resources available to them, students will be able to compile data about their own site's ecological conditions using many of the same resources. Data about some of the site's abiotic characteristics, especially humidity and rainfall, can be compiled by having students monitor local weather statistics found among print and electronic media. Various government agencies, such as the National Oceanic and Atmospheric Administration (NOAA) provide data that can be accessed via the Internet, and local and regional weather bureaus can be contacted directly for daily statistics. The Resources List on page 58 provides website addresses for some of these information sources.

For temperature measurements, have one student in each group record temperatures at ground level, a second student record temperatures at approximately one meter above ground level, and a third student record temperatures at two meters above ground level.

To measure wind speed, construct a simple anemometer. Cut a small notch about 20 mm from one end of a smooth clear drinking straw, and make a pinhole about 35 mm from the other end (on the same side as the notch). Plug the straw's notch-end with modeling clay. This will be the bottom of the instrument. Use a piece of 25 mm–thick Styrofoam (80 x 200 mm) to form a base. Place a Styrofoam ball, small enough to fit loosely, into the straw. Center the straw on the cardboard with both notch and pinhole facing up. The top of the straw should extend 20 mm beyond the cardboard's edge. Insert one pin 30 mm from the bottom of the straw and one pin 10 mm below the pinhole. The pins will both trap the ball and attach the straw firmly to the base. To calibrate, hold the anemometer (vertically and facing the wind) out the window of a car. Use a pencil to mark the position of the Styrofoam ball in the straw, at various speeds.

For the purposes of this activity, sunlight can be quantified in terms of sunny, partly sunny, and not sunny at specific areas. Make sure students take note of changes in shade conditions among the site's various areas.

Figure 2
The marten is a threatened top predator indigenous to the Pacific Northwest. Like the spotted owl, it also relies on old-growth forest habitat to meet its biological requirements.

6. Have the groups studying inhabitant species each examine a different area within the study site. Different species may enter different areas at different times, so students should remain at the site throughout the activity. Remind them that they will need to be as unobtrusive as possible so as not to disturb the site's wildlife. Have each group create a list of the species they observe. Remind them not to overlook insects and birds. You may also wish them to hypothesize about species likely to inhabit the area when humans are not present. (For example, nocturnal animals would not be present during the activity, and species like rabbits and deer might have been scared away.)

7. When the groups have finished recording data, return to the classroom. Have the entire class generate a map of the site. You may wish to have the entire class' input on what should be included on the map, but have only one "artist" draw it. Then you can copy and distribute identical maps to each student. Note: Be sure to include and mark the areas within the site at which measurements were recorded.

8. Using a variety of colored pencils, have each group show areas that have similar data. For example, the group that studied local vegetation could use a light green pencil to shade the areas with low grass, a dark green pencil to depict high grass, black to represent a forested area, and yellow to show scrub grass. Each group should make its own map to represent the variations they found. Note: For temperature measurements, use a different colored pencil for measurements taken at ground level, at one meter, and at two meters.

Part B: Assessing Habitat Loss

In Part B, students use math skills to calculate the impact of habitat loss on a model spotted owl population. Students first calculate normal fluctuations among that population, and then add the variable of habitat loss to their calculations in order to assess its impact.

While ecologists conducting advanced studies of ecosystem dynamics and population fluctuations incorporate many kinds of variables into their calculations, the fundamental mathematical process they all use is based on the equations students use in this activity. Students should be encouraged to appreciate that they are engaging in a "real-world" scientific activity applicable to ecological conditions and population dynamics on a broad scale. Note: for the purposes of this activity, figures will be rounded up or down to the nearest whole number.

Materials
Photocopies of the Northern Spotted Owl Information Sheet (pages 38 and 39)

Procedure

1. Assume you are beginning with a total owl population of 100 nesting owls with 50 males and 50 females. To calculate the total number of owls produced per year, first calculate the number of female young produced per year. Multiply the number of females (50) by the number of female young produced per female per year (0.548), or:

$$50 \times 0.548 = 27.4 \text{ or } 27$$

At a 50:50 female-to-male ratio, the number of males produced per year is equal to the number of females produced per year, or 27. The total number of owls produced per year equals the number of females produced per year plus the number of males produced per year, or:

$$27 + 27 = 54$$

2. To calculate the total number of owls produced per year that would survive their first year, multiply the total number of owls produced per year (54) by the owl population survival rate (0.143), or:

$$54 \times 0.143 = 7.7 \text{ or } 8$$

To calculate the number of owls produced per year that would not survive their first year, subtract the number of owls produced per year that would survive their first year from the total number of owls produced per year (54), or:

$$54 - 8 = 46$$

Teaching Note
You may want to discuss the Spotted Owl Population Information from page 39 with students, and display it on the chalkboard or overhead, before going through the procedure and calculations. Then photocopy pages 38 and 39 for distribution to students or small groups. The Owl Population Dynamics table is the "answer" to the successive calculations in this procedure, but students should be encouraged to see the calculations as a tool, not as a math exercise.

Northern Spotted Owl

The Northern Spotted Owl, *Strix occidentalis caurina*

Size: Length from 400–500 mm. Wingspread up to 1,200 mm. Female is the larger.

Characteristics: Uses a wide range of sounds, such as hoots, screeches, and wails. Hunts at night using "silent flight" to swoop in on prey. Eats prey whole and regurgitates pellets of fur, bones, and feathers. Large eyes for good night vision. Eyes are immovable. Exellent hearing. Head swivels in order to lock onto sounds and sights. Female has no ear tufts.

Color: Overall cover is chestnut. White and brown spots on underparts and breast. Chestnut tail feathers with lighter brown and white markings.

Behavior: Nocturnal. Lives in old-growth forests. Uses trees for protection against predators and for nesting.

Reproduction and lifespan: Does not build nests; uses broken trees or tree cavities.

Wild diet: Carnivorous, eats rodents, shrews, small animals. Stores excess food and retrieves later.

Zoo diet: Chicks, mice, and bird-of-prey diet.

Status: Threatened.

Habitat and range: Pacific Northwest. There are four types of owl habitats, those for nesting, roosting, foraging, and dispersal of young.

What are the spotted owl's habitat requirements?

When it comes to suitable habitat for the northern spotted owl, a forest's structure and composition are more important than its actual age. Scientific research shows that spotted owls will use a wide variety of forest types for foraging, including a fragmented habitat. In its northern range, the owls often choose large, dense forests for foraging, probably because such forests contain large populations of the owl's favorite food, the northern flying squirrel. The flying squirrel eats mostly fungal material, the kind that grows in the upper canopy of an old-growth forest. In its southern range, spotted owls will forage along the edges of dense forests and in more open or fragmented forests.

A suitable nesting and roosting habitat for spotted owls includes a moderate to high canopy closure (60–80 percent closure); a multi-layered, multi-species canopy with large, overstory trees; many large trees with various kinds of deformities; large accumulations of fallen trees and other kinds of debris; and sufficient open space below the canopy for them to fly around. A nesting pair of spotted owls requires about 1.3 km² of late-successional second-growth or virgin old-growth forest to meet their habitat requirements.

About 75 percent of the known population of spotted owls lives on federal lands. Spotted owl site centers on non-federal lands exist primarily in old-growth forests and in late-successional second-growth forests that contain the ecological conditions described above. As of July 1994, there were 851 sites with resident single owls or pairs in Washington State. Of these, 140 sites are on non-federal lands. An additional 151 sites partially depend on adjacent non-federal lands to support their spotted owls.

Information Sheet

Spotted Owl Population Information

Number of female young produced per female per year:	0.548
Annual survival rates for first year:	0.143
Proportion of young emigrating:	0.40
Annual survival rates for all later years:	0.86
Crude density (number of individuals per hectare):	0.0152

All values come from *Viability Assessments and Management Con-siderations for Species Associated with Late-Successional and Old-Growth Forests of the Pacific Northwest.* 1993. USDA.

Owl Population Dynamics

Year	Number of Owls	Number of Females	Number of Young	Number of Young Survivors	Number of Non-emigrants	Number of Adult Survivors	Total Number of Owls Surviving
Year 1	100	50	54	8	5	86	91
Year 2	91	45	50	7	4	78	82
Year 3	82	41	44	8	5	71	76
Year 4	76	38	42	7	4	65	69
Year 5	69	34	37	5	3	59	62

Why is there so much debate about the spotted owl ?

The northern spotted owl is considered an *indicator species* because it feeds at the top trophic level in old-growth forest food webs. If the owl is threatened, this indicates that dozens of other species are probably also at risk. The U.S. Fish and Wildlife Service added the northern spotted owl to the federal list of threatened species in 1990. Because of this, the owl's old-growth forest habitat is protected from logging, or any other practices that would hurt its chances for survival.

This federal decision may have been good for the spotted owl, but the Northern Pacific timber industry says it hurt the region's economy by raising lumber prices at least 30 percent. The timber industry has since been trying to persuade Congress to take economic factors into consideration when it classifies a species as threatened, and they want Congress to decrease the amount of federally protected old-growth habitat.

Everybody agrees there is a need to balance resource conservation with economic growth. But the question is: Just what *is* an old-growth habitat? How old does a forest have to be before it becomes old-growth? A hundred years? Two hundred years? Three hundred years? It's an important question because the average human lifespan is about 75 years. If federal regulations were to require, for example, that newly planted trees be left undisturbed for 200 years, then timber companies couldn't harvest and market their products inside any kind of economically viable timeframe. That's why many of them want the definition of "old-growth" to be around 100 years.

The distinction makes a difference, both to a forest's inhabitant species and to the Northern Pacific economy. Loggers, millworkers, and store owners who live in these communities are caught in the middle. They fear that further restrictions on available land could cost them their jobs. Yet logging out old-growth forests could also cost jobs, because automation and exporting raw logs increases deforestation rates.

How can this be resolved? Would kinds of evidence should decisions be based on? How can different kinds of evidence from different sources—like economics and science—be linked to address such problems?

3. Assume that, of the surviving owls, 40 percent emigrate. To calculate the number of owls that remain, multiply the number of surviving owls (8) by 40 percent (0.40), or:

$$8 \times 0.40 = 3.2 \text{ or } 3$$

This means that three owls would emigrate and five would remain.

4. For the original 50 pairs of nesting owls, if the annual survivorship rate is 0.143 then the number of adult owls surviving in a given year is equal to the number of nesting owls (100) times the annual survivorship rate (0.86), or:

$$100 \times 0.86 = 86$$

Adding the number of adult owls surviving (86) to the number of young survivors remaining (5) provides the total number of owls in the model owl population, or:

$$86 + 5 = 91$$

This figure (91) represents the total number of owls—the owl population—that rely on the model old-growth forest habitat to meet their biological needs.

5. It may be necessary to have students work through these computations (steps 1–4) several times in order to establish a degree of comfort with the way they work. While the equations themselves are not overly complicated, they do require a certain amount of attentiveness in order to keep focused. It may be helpful to point out to students that each numerical equation can be easily described using ordinary language. Have them try this, using the language in steps 1–4 as a model.

6. Once students understand this relationship between numbers and words, have them turn their attention to the Owl Population Dynamics table on their photocopies (page 39). Encourage them to locate the numbers with which they have been working among the numbers on the table. For example, they should be able to recognize and identify each of the numbers they used in their calculations along the top row of numbers.

7. After they have successfully identified each number, turn student attention to the headings above each of the vertical columns. In this way, students will have a graphic representation directly in front of them depicting the relationship between words and numbers. Tell students that this is the process ecologists use to describe population dynamics for all species among all Earth's ecosystems.

8. Now tell students that, having calculated the size of the model old-growth forest habitat's owl population for one year, they will now calculate how much of that forest habitat this model owl population requires to meet its biological needs. To do this, divide the total number of owls (100 owls, 91 owls, and so forth) by the crude density estimate (0.0152 individuals/hectare) to obtain the minimum amount of old-growth forest habitat required to meet the owl population's biological needs, or:

$$100/0.0152 = 6{,}579 \text{ hectares, or } 65.79 \text{ km}^2$$

Thus, 100 owls (50 nesting pairs) require a minimum habitat area of 65.79 km^2 of old-growth forest to meet their biological needs.

9. To demonstrate to students how habitat loss can affect this model owl population, have them recall the reference grids they created for activity 1 part B (page 10) when they explored change in the Olympic Peninsula's forest ecosystem. First, have students calculate the minimum habitat required for the dwindling owl population. Now have them create a table using the figures they derive, as depicted below.

Conversion Note
Students may not be able to readily visualize a hectare (ha) or a square kilometer (km^2). You may want to also write on the board that:

1 ha = 10,000 m^2, which is a square with sides 100 meters long

1 km^2 = 1,000,000 m^2, which is a square with sides 1,000 meters long

100 ha = 1 km^2

Total Number of Owls	Minimum Habitat Required
100	65.79 km^2
91	59.87 km^2
82	53.95 km^2
76	50.00 km^2
69	45.39 km^2

10. Now have students compare the figures they derived in step 9 with the figures for total remaining forested area they derived using their reference grids. Lead a general discussion about the impact of habitat loss on inhabitant species.

Questions for Discussion

Part A

1. Lead a class discussion about the organisms students observed. Ask students what they think these organisms require for a healthy life. Have students list environmental characteristics they think would be most suitable for these organisms.

2. Have students research the organisms they observed in field guides and compare the organisms' habitat needs with the data they collected in the field. Encourage them to consider such questions as: How are the needs of different organisms similar? How are they different? Is this habitat "suitable" for the organisms living there? Why or why not?

3. Discuss the variations students observed among different areas within the site. Ask students how such variations affect the area's inhabitant species. On what do they base their responses?

4. Present students with this scenario: A local developer constructs a paved road straight through the site. What impact might the road have on the site's suitability for its inhabitant species?

5. Have students develop a definition of habitat, provide examples, and present them to the class. You may wish to have the class take the best part of each to derive the best possible overall definition of habitat.

6. Ask students how they think deforestation might impact endangered species.

Part B

1. Ask students to explain the difference in survivorship among young and adult owls.

2. Density estimates don't reflect individual differences. Ask students if they would expect different owls to require differently-sized habitats. Have them give specific examples and explain why.

3. The calculations show how many owls emigrated, but they don't reflect any immigration. Ask students to consider how emigration and immigration might be affected by the presence or absence of wildlife corridors. Invite them to provide specific examples.

Answers to Discussion Questions

Part A

1. All organisms will require energy, water, space, a suitable climate, and nutrients. The specific ecological details of a particular organism's requirements will vary among both locations and species.

2. Answers will vary, but organism needs should fit within the basic categories outlined in answer #1.

3. Diverse study sites should produce variations in such abiotic factors as temperature, humidity, wind, and nutrient availability. By comparing the needs of organisms with such variations, students should be able to assess the suitability of different areas within the study site for different organisms.

4. If the study site is wooded, removal of trees will result in changes in its abiotic components. These abiotic changes will in turn have an impact on the site's biotic components, such as its inhabitant species. Organisms preferring cooler, moister, shaded conditions, for example, will be subjected to changes in temperature, humidity, and sunlight.

5. Student answers will vary, but should include the parameters required by an organism for its survival.

6. Deforestation will result in the removal or outright destruction of a forest habitat's abiotic and biotic components. Inhabitant species will have to relocate, adjust, or perish.

Part B

1. Young owls may be more susceptible to disease and predation than adult owls. Also, if one or both of a nesting pair are killed, the young owls' chance of survival is significantly reduced.

2. Larger animals usually require a larger habitat area to meet their biological needs. Breeding pairs and pairs with young also require larger habitat area.

3. Wildlife corridors can aid the movement of owls from one habitat area to another. Such corridors can also enable immigration and emigration to and from habitat areas.

Government Land-Use Designations and their Meanings

The United States Government has an extensive system of public lands, and all of them are classified according to their use and the management techniques that are applied to them. For example, some public lands are designated for use by humans while others are designated to be left undisturbed. In general, the difference between how public lands are designated depends on the degree to which humans may use them. Here is a general outline of federal land-use designations.

National Parks—Administered by the U.S. National Park Service (NPS), a division of the U.S. Department of the Interior. America's national parks comprise about 18,800,000 hectares. The first National Park, Yellowstone, was created in 1872. In 1916, Congress passed the Organic Act to "conserve the scenery and the natural and historical objects and wildlife therein, and to provide for the enjoyment of the same in such manner as will leave them unimpaired for the enjoyment of future generations."

National Forests—Administered by the U.S. Forest Service (USFS), a division of the U.S. Department of Agriculture. America's national forests comprise about 76,400,000 hectares. National forests are designated for multiple purposes, both commercial and recreational. Loggers and miners, ranchers, and tourism and campground operators are among the commercial enterprises that purchase leases and concessions directly from the Forest Service. The Forest Bureau, later upgraded to Service status, was created by act of Congress in 1902.

National Resource Lands—Administered by the Bureau of Land Management (BLM), a division of the U.S. Department of the Interior. Used for grazing, mining, and logging, the total area managed by the BLM comprises 136,400,000 hectares, mostly in the western states and Alaska. They consist of public lands *not* designated for use as recreational, defense, university land grants, or otherwise. The BLM was formed in 1946 when two government land-management agencies were merged together.

National Wildlife Refuge—Administered by the U.S. Fish and Wildlife Service (FWS), a division of the U.S. Department of the Interior. Comprises 36,000,000 million hectares, of which 5,200,000 are in Alaska. The FWS was created in 1966 to "provide, preserve, restore, and manage a national network of lands and waters sufficient in size, diversity, and location to meet society's needs for areas where the widest spectrum of benefits associated with wildlife and wild lands is enhanced and made available." No commercial logging.

National Wilderness Preservation System—Comprises 35,440,000 hectares of national forest, national park, BLM, and wildlife refuge lands in the continental United States and Alaska. While use of wilderness areas is heavily regulated, "grandfathered" mining rights continue in some areas. No commercial logging.

National Wild and Scenic Rivers and National Trails Systems—Established in 1968, its primary purpose is for recreation and the preservation of natural beauty. The system comprises 11,632.25 kilometers of water along 66 designated rivers and river segments which are to be kept "forever free of development," including dredging, damming, and filling. Each segment is administered by the government agency whose land it borders.

Native American Lands—Lands occupied by Native American peoples are designated "tribal lands," and are not administered by federal or state governments. They are not technically private lands, in that they are tax exempt and they sometimes receive federal support for their upkeep and management.

State Lands—Each of the 50 United States owns and manages lands designated for a variety of uses, especially recreational. Contact your state government for free information about how it manages its public lands.

Adapted from Zaslowsky, D. 1986. *These American Lands*. Washington, D.C. The Wilderness Society.

Suggestions for Further Study

• Have students collect and analyze habitat data for an indoor habitat, such as their classroom. Open doors and windows to increase the diversity of micro-climates within the classroom.

• Have students consider the question: Who cares? What difference does it make if northern spotted owls or martens become extinct? It may be helpful for students to approach these questions by framing their answers in terms of scientific, economic, aesthetic, and ethical considerations and then comparing and contrasting their answers. Encourage them to weigh pertinent information derived from each approach, and then frame a comprehensive answer. Students may want to conduct research on the national debate over threatened and endangered species, and then hold their own debate.

• Contact the U.S. Environmental Protection Agency and ask for a copy of the most current endangered species list. Have students study the list to identify other species for study. Students may wish to form small groups, research a particular endangered species, and create present-ations to share their findings with the entire class. Encourage students to consider various different formats for their presentation, such as a skit, art exhibit, or debate. They may wish to combine several different formats to enhance the effectiveness—and fun—of their presentations.

• Have students identify various key words pertaining to the subject of habitat loss and its impact on inhabitant species, perhaps derived from their study of the endangered species list. If your school has computer resources available, have students use the key words they identify to "surf the net" and see what they come up with. The Internet is an excellent resource for exploring environmental change topics and issues, and provides a platform for launching many interesting areas of study. It is also an excellent way to integrate information from pertinent disciplines, especially among the physical and social sciences. See the Resources List beginning on page 58 for some website addresses to use as starting points.

• Have students look up the words *preservation* and *conservation* and compare and contrast their definitions. Invite them to address the question: Is it possible to leave a habitat entirely undisturbed by humans, considering the fact that human-induced, wind- and water-borne pollutants circumnavigate the Earth?

Understanding Land Use

Background

Objective
To understand how federal land-use decisions affect different groups by developing an Environmental Impact Statement.

The Federal Government is legally required to evaluate the environmental impact of any action it proposes. This evaluation process involves several stages. First, in an environmental impact assessment, government scientists conduct a broad assessment of the proposed action's environmental impact. If, after conducting this broad assessment, they think a more detailed scientific study is needed, then they present their evidence to Congress to secure funding. Once the more detailed study is completed, and if they decide that the proposed action *will* have an environmental impact, they conduct an even more detailed, in-depth analysis in order to generate substantive proposals and alternatives for minimizing these impacts. This is an Environmental Impact Statement (EIS).

Teaching Note
Information about the EIS process and the Congressional National Environmental Policy Act (NEPA) can be found through the EPA's home page: http:\\www.epa.gov

An EIS assesses the proposed action's impact on the environment—water, air, and soil quality; natural systems including rivers, forests, wilderness, and other areas; and individual species. It also addresses impacts on the economies and cultures of local communities. For example, would the action adversely affect a national historic site? Would it cost local citizens their jobs? Would people need to relocate?

Once a draft EIS is prepared, it is made available to the public for review, comment, and criticism. The EIS authors are legally required to address any and all public feedback before publishing a final EIS. Finally, the government publishes a Record of Decision, which officially records the action it will undertake. This document contains specific measures designed to minimize the environmental, economic, and cultural impacts of its action. The measures are derived from a broad range of sources—especially the physical and social sciences—and the input of a wide variety of citizens, groups, and public and private concerns is weighed and given a voice. The process is complex but democratic, because it ensures that all interests who want it have a say before any government project begins.

Time Management
This role-play activity can be organized in various ways, depending on how much time you have allotted and if you want to use class time for student research. Part C can take 1–2 periods, depending on class size and presentation length.

This role-play activity is designed to help students understand how this process works. It does this by paralleling the procedure the U.S. Federal Government uses to create a forest management plan. Your students will assume the roles of scientists, economists, policymakers, and citizens as they work through this activity. Working together—both within their own groups and as groups—they will examine and assess various land-use proposals, possibilities, and alternatives. They will conduct research in order to gather information and compile data from pertinent sources, and they will weigh the merits of the information and data they collect. They will also weigh the interests of people who will be affected by the proposed action, and consider the ecological, economic, and cultural impacts that an action might have.

In Part A, the class will be divided into groups, and each group will decide what kinds of data it needs to support its position (as outlined in their Group Profile). Each group will then conduct research to gather information and compile data. In Part B, each group will develop its own land-use proposal, which must be supported by their research, and then make a formal (uninterrupted) presentation of its proposal to the entire class. In Part C, the class will hold a formal debate to evaluate the pros and cons of the various proposals, and then work together to create a final draft of an Environmental Impact Statement.

Materials
Previous activities
Large paper sheets
Felt markers
Other art supplies, as needed
1 copy of each Group Profile (pages 50–53)
4 copies of the Student Information Pack (pages 54–57)
4 copies of the Resources List, optional (pages 58–61)

Procedure

Part A: Gathering Information

1. Tell students they are about to begin an extended project concerning United States environmental policy. Tell them they will be integrating knowledge and skills they have acquired from previous activities, as well as from other sources, toward developing an Environmental Impact Statement to determine how old-growth forest within Washington State's Olympic Peninsula is to be used. Tell students they will play roles, which means they might have to assume a position they don't necessarily agree with. While they are to play a role consistent with their Group Profile, they should feel free to add to it in any way they feel is appropriate (such as dressing the part). They will work in groups to research and design the "best" land-use proposal, they will present their proposals to the class, and all the groups will work together to create a final land-use plan for the old-growth forest in the Olympic Peninsula. Every step of their decision-making process will be presided over by a Federal Judge, their teacher.

Class Organization
Each group will decide the roles it needs its individual students to play in order to most effectively gather information, make presentations, and hold debate. The groups should be encouraged to alter and change these roles as they learn more about what they need. Before creating each group, you may want to consider how a particular collection of personalities within a group might affect this process.

Teaching Note
As the Judge you will, of course, want to monitor the groups' ongoing progress as they gather information and compile data. The time you allot for this process may depend on how successful the groups are in conducting their research, but you may want to impose a deadline for completing Part A. Deadlines do exist in the "real-world" EIS evaluation process, and this might add an interesting component to this activity.

2. Divide the class into four groups, and give each group a copy of a particular Group Profile. Also give each group a copy of the Student Information Packet and a copy of the Resources List (optional). Alternatively, you can provide each individual student within each group with their own copies of these materials, but it might prove interesting to see how each group coordinates the use of just one set. What provisions for sharing, or copying, do they create?

3. Have the groups read through their profiles and, drawing on what they've learned from previous activities and other sources, discuss amongst themselves what the objectives of their group should be. After making a list of their objectives, they should decide what kinds of information they might need to effectively create a land-use proposal that furthers those objectives. Have them list roles for individuals, or for smaller focus groups, to adopt within their particular group and show them to the Judge for possible clarification, direction, or revision.

4. Have each group conduct research to gather information and compile data that supports and furthers its particular objectives. As they do so, the groups may revise and alter their roles and research directions to address pertinent areas of study. Have the groups advise the Judge of any alterations as they consider making them.

Part B: Developing Proposals

1. Once the groups have finished their research, you may want to have them develop an outline of how they intend to make use of it. This may be done either in or outside of class, and provides the Judge with an opportunity to (a) monitor each group's intentions before the debate and (b) assess and evaluate each group's progress as the activity unfolds. Groups will need to know how much time they have to present their proposals; a specific amount of time should be allotted for each presentation, such as 10 or 15 minutes.

2. Have each group develop a research-based land-use proposal that addresses their particular objectives. Groups may be allowed some latitude with regard to creativity in how they choose to document their proposal. Depending on the resources available to them, students may wish to combine a variety of different formats—such as video, three-dimensional models, artwork, and skits—in documenting their own proposals. How the groups choose to organize their material in preparing their presentations might also provide the Judge with a means for assessing and evaluating their overall performance.

3. Have each group present its proposal to the entire class. These should be uninterrupted presentations, but you may want to allow for a brief question-and-answer period either at the end of each presentation or after all presentations have been concluded. As each group makes its presentation, non-presenting groups should be encouraged to take notes in preparation for the upcoming debate.

4. Depending on the amount of time you have allotted for this activity, the groups may want to revise their proposals after having heard the proposals of other groups, or in light of the strengths and weaknesses that emerged during the question-and-answer period(s). When this is completed, proceed to Part C.

Part C: Debate and Decision

1. Hold a class debate to evaluate the pros and cons of the various old-growth forest land-use proposals. Depending on your class size and dynamics, this debate may be organized in a variety of ways. One way is to have each group select an individual or team to represent it in a formal debate. Another way is for the Judge to preside over a more general class discussion. Yet another way is to adopt a "town meeting" approach, with group representatives sitting at a dais. Other ways of conducting this debate may present themselves upon discussion with the class, or as adapted from information gathered during the groups' researches. Regardless, students should be polite and courteous to one another, and bear in mind that they are participating in a democratic decision-making process.

2. As the debate unfolds, have students add to their existing notes regarding the pros and cons of the land-use proposals under consideration. Remind them that they must agree as a class on a land-use plan, but this doesn't necessarily mean they must adopt a particular proposal in its entirety. The best elements from each proposal should be considered and combined in creating their final Environmental Impact Statement.

3. Have the class draft its final Environmental Impact Statement for the Olympic Peninsula's old-growth forests. This will require teamwork, cooperation, and compromise. Encourage the class to base its final land-use decision on information and data it has gathered and merged during the course of this activity.

Assessment Note
Many opportunities for assessment and evaluation present themselves during the course of this activity. One of the most significant, however, is how well students work together, both within their particular groups and with other groups. In the "real world" of environmental debate, conflict resolution often involves compromise.

The Native American League

Your group comprises Native American peoples who live on the four reservations on the Olympic Peninsula. Your reservations lie at the estuaries of the Peninsula's four primary riverways. Both traditional and contemporary links between Pacific Northwest Native American peoples and forest ecosystems make it clear that tribal members depend on natural resources for employment, subsistence, and cultural identity.

Your primary sources of income are, therefore, directly connected to the area's forest ecosystem, so any land-use plan that affects this ecosystem also affects you. Many of the people you represent have jobs with the Xylem Timber Company, but some of them also work for the various federal agencies that administer public lands on the Peninsula. Some of your people derive a significant part of their income from the ecosystem's inhabitant species, especially the salmon that breed in the rivers.

Within the past several decades, and especially in the past few years, the annual salmon harvest has declined noticeably. Many people are growing extremely concerned about this, and they think it could be a result of the increased rate of deforestation in the upland areas. How do the current logging practices that are being used upriver affect the salmons' breeding grounds? If those practices are changed, how might this affect people who have jobs with the Xylem Timber Company? Although many of your people do earn a good living, it's true that the region's economy isn't doing as well as most people would like.

Some of the people you represent think it might be a good idea for all the tribes to return to a more traditional lifestyle, one that doesn't depend so much on the region's logging economy for employment and income. Also, there may be other sources of income that would be worth exploring. Many people, such as those who live in cities, like to spend leisure time in forests. Such people are especially interested in the diversity of the area's biological species. How might the tribes be able to capitalize on this?

But not everyone feels this way, and some tribal families have held jobs in the logging industry for several generations. There are important questions about cultural identity being discussed among the tribes. How can the Native American people who live on the Olympic Peninsula raise their standard of living while still maintaining their sense of who they are?

Everyone among your League does agree that this is a critical time for all the tribes. The decisions that get made today about how the forest will be used are going to have a dramatic effect on future generations, on your children. So it's particularly important that the proposal you create be backed by strong supporting evidence.

The Xylem Timber Company

Your group operates a logging operation in the Olympic Peninsula, and has done so since the late 1800s. You own large tracts of continuous, uninterrupted forest on the Peninsula, and you use a variety of different techniques to manage the tree species there. Since the early 1900s, you have had considerable success with sustained-yield forestry practices. Your stockholders want a steady source of income, and sustained-yield forest management provides this.

You employ many of the people who live in the northwest Washington State region, and you would employ even more if you could extend your logging operations into areas that contain late-successional second-growth and old-growth trees. After logging those areas, you want to apply sustained-yield techniques to them too.

Your company has good contacts among people who work for the various federal agencies in the area, and you have a good track record for working with them and complying with federal environmental regulations. You are keenly aware that these federal agencies have been instructed by the President of the United States to work together to develop a land-use proposal for the Olympic Peninsula, and that anything you do—or don't do—might therefore be covered by the national news media.

You also have strong ties to the Native American communities in the area. Recently though, some of these communities have expressed concern that your logging practices upriver might be affecting their salmon fisheries. How can you help create a land-use proposal that continues to earn profits for your stockholders, continues to support the region's economy by providing jobs, and doesn't have a negative effect on those natural resources that Native American people—and others—rely on for their livelihoods?

For the past 25 years, many people who don't live on the Olympic Peninsula—and some who do—have been trying to put a stop to your logging operations, or at least to slow them down. You are aware that the public's perception of what timber companies do isn't as good as it could be. And it costs time and money to always be on the defensive. Because of this, you view this situation as an opportunity. How, if at all, could you change your current practices to improve your public relations? If you did find a way to accomplish this, would it cost people their jobs and hurt the region's economy? How would stockholders react? Some people have recently bought stock in your company because they want to change the way you extract timber, and owning stock means they have a say in what you do. These people, some of whom have connections with environmental groups, are particularly interested in preserving habitat for the region's diverse biological species, but they have other concerns as well. How can you achieve a balance between conserving the region's natural resources and helping its economy to grow? How can you work with others to create a land-use plan everyone can agree on?

The Federal Agencies Group

Your group is comprised of people who work for the various federal land-management agencies that administer public lands in the Olympic Peninsula, especially the Bureau of Land Management, the Forest Service, the National Park Service, and the Fish and Wildlife Service. Recently the President of the United States instructed all of these federal agencies to work together to create a land-use proposal for the Olympic Peninsula. Federal law requires you to take into consideration the opinions and concerns of a wide variety of people from a broad range of interests, such as logging companies, Native American and other local residents, environmental concerns, the scientific community, and others.

You also have a broader responsibility to the public interest. The ecosystems for which you are responsible are the property of the American people, and there are many American citizens who think that these ecosystems should be made available to the public only for recreational purposes, such as camping and hunting. But there are other people, also American citizens, who think these areas should be used only to earn money, such as from mining and logging. Other citizens think that a great portion of the region should be closed off to humans so that the biological species that inhabit the area will be left undisturbed. Still other citizens think it's possible to reach a compromise that allows for recreation, preservation, and profit. How can you help all these different interest groups work together to develop a land-use proposal that balances resource conservation with economic growth?

As federal agencies, you have access to a great amount of scientific data, all of which is public information. To learn more about the data your group has, ask the Judge for a copy of page 44, "Government Land-Use Designations and their Meanings." This will tell you more about some of the agencies in your group.

The federal government itself uses some of these lands to earn money, especially by leasing rights to timber and mining companies, and selling licenses to people who want to hunt and fish. Both federal and state governments also earn money from companies that operate campgrounds, restaurants, tours, and many other recreation-related activites. The money that governments earn this way is called a "concession," and the companies that pay concessions are called "concessionaires."

There are a variety of different ways that you might try to help coordinate this land-use proposal process, but you should be aware that there *are* people who don't necessarily appreciate being told what to do by the federal government, even if you're trying to help. The main thing is to work well together amongst yourselves. Maybe you can lead by example if you are successful.

SaveOlympic!

Your group is a consortium of various environmental concerns. A few of these concerns are regional—meaning they are concerned mostly with what happens in western Washington State and the Olympic Peninsula—but some are national and even international. These concerns are interested in a broad range of environmental issues around the world, but they are especially interested in preserving ecosystems that play an important role in global ecological processes. But, regardless of your individual concerns and objectives, you all want to see as much as possible of the Olympic Peninsula's old-growth forest ecosystem left undisturbed.

You have been active in helping create land-use plans for a variety of different ecosystem types since the 1970s, and you've been pretty successful in mobilizing public opinion to support your causes over the years. However, the tactics you have traditionally relied on for this have become less effective. You think this is probably due to several factors, such as a better educated public and better defenses from the people whose practices you've tried to halt. Whatever the reason, you want to use the current situation to try to develop new approaches and broaden your support base.

One way might be to support your objectives with as much scientific evidence as you can find. Also, in order for this process to work effectively, the other groups will need to feel as though most of their objectives have been met. Your group views this as an opportunity to work together with other interested parties—especially timber companies and federal agencies—to create a land-use proposal for the Olympic Peninsula that will serve as a model for saving other endangered ecosystems. To do this, you will need to find a way to conserve the Pacific Northwest's natural resources while still allowing for their use. How will you do this?

You have a lot of experience with other forest ecosystems around the world, so you can demonstrate scientifically how deforestation affects ecological processes and biological relationships. How does deforestation affect rivers and estuaries? What does it do to biogeochemical cycling and energy flow? What evidence can you assemble to show how species are affected? What is the role of old-growth forests in global ecological processes, and why is it important?

Background Information

The old-growth forests of the Olympic Peninsula have been logged commercially ever since the first non-native peoples began arriving in the interior valleys of western Washington State. Old-growth forest covered much of the landscape there, and it was initially viewed by arriving immigrants as an impediment to settlement, farming, and livestock grazing. As a result of this widely held view, forested areas were systematically cleared, mostly by burning.

By the late 1800s, timber extraction for commercial purposes had dramatically increased, and lumber camps sprang up around the region, especially near riverways and railroad depots. Early logging techniques consisted mostly of clear cutting and burning, and little attention was paid to replanting young trees or reseeding logged out areas. A seemingly inexhaustible supply of trees and the enormous amount of physical labor required to fell and extract them contributed to wasteful practices.

But people were beginning to become concerned about how America's natural resources were being used. By the turn of the 19th century, groups such as the American Forestry Association and the National Preservation Society were lobbying Congress to enact legislation requiring more sustainable uses of rapidly depleting resources, especially trees. During the Progressive Era—roughly 1895 to 1915—the Legislative and Executive branches of the United States Government did work to pass laws requiring better timber harvesting practices. Federal agencies such as the Bureau of Land Management, the U.S. Forest Service, and the National Park Service were created to regulate natural resource use.

Of course, there was considerable debate about how these new laws would be upheld and which government agencies would regulate them. In fact, the present debate about United States environmental policy has much in common with that earlier debate. Logging did continue, however, with the result that today the forests of the Pacific Northwest—such as the ones you will be developing land-use proposals for in this activity—consist of a highly fragmented mosaic of old-growth and late-successional second-growth stands, recent clear cuts, thinned-out stands, and young tree plantations interspersed with uncut natural stands.

During the early 20th century, the new science of ecology began studying how ecosystems work. Ecology combined areas of study from many branches of science, especially biology, botany, and physics. But always ecologists were thinking about how ecosystems might be managed sustainably in order to get the most out of them for human use while still allowing them to function. The intricate relationship between animals, plants, and humans—known as the food web—became the model.

Increased knowledge about the way ecosystems work—and about the role of forests in Earth's ecological processes—has led to an increased concern about what's happening to old-growth forests, especially those in the Pacific Northwest. As scientific evidence has accumulated, it has become increasingly apparent that once these unique old-growth ecosystems are logged for their timber they will probably be gone forever, along with the many biological species that rely on them for their habitat requirements. But if a halt to timber extraction is put into effect, then human economies that have grown up in these areas will suffer and many people might lose their jobs. How can we balance resource conservation with economic growth?

That is the question you must debate and answer in this role-playing activity. In the box below, you will find a brief description of actual events that led to the creation of current United States environmental policy for this area. As you read about these events, keep in mind that the United States is a democracy: this means that everyone should have a say in what happens on public lands, and that the final decision will be a compromise. This is important to remember as you work with other groups to decide what to do with the Olympic Peninsula's old-growth forests.

History of the EPA's Record of Decision for the Pacific Northwest

The Pacific Northwest is a valuable national asset. It contains most of the last remnants of old growth forests, supports a diversity of life, and contributes to ecological stability both locally and globally. The area also supports a significant timber industry. As a result, tension between conservation and economic interests has increased over the last decades. The logging industry fears further regulation of federal land will reduce jobs and profits; the conservation community is sure that unrestricted logging will result in the total, permanent loss of old-growth forest and rare species.

Seeking a compromise, President Clinton convened the Forest Conference in April, 1993 in Portland, Oregon. After the conference, the president appointed a team to develop a management policy for federal lands in the Pacific Northwest and northern California. The team included scientists, economists, sociologists, and others from various federal agencies. After a three-month investigation, the team released an Environmental Impact Statement containing 10 options for managing the forests. All 10 options balanced economic needs with conservation interests. The options assessed how much and what kind of habitat was needed by the region's endangered species; how rivers would be affected by future logging; and how much old growth forest could be preserved.

The Department of Agriculture and the Department of the Interior then jointly published a document explaining which option they chose. This Record of Decision was released in April, 1994. In essence, the decision is a long-term plan for sustaining both the Pacific Northwest's natural resources and its timber industry.

The plan allows limited logging of old-growth areas by setting rules about the level of logging in a variety of designated areas. Late successional stands, especially those near watersheds, receive the most protection. The plan also protects about 80 percent of the area inhabited by endangered species such as the northern spotted owl. Some regions of the forest are designated as "adaptive management areas." These areas will be extensively monitored to see how land use affects their ecosystems. Observations of adaptive management areas will show if the government needs to adjust its management policies.

The Situation

In Washington State's Olympic Peninsula, the Olympic National Park Coastal Strip stretches 10 kilometers in width and 50 kilometers in length. Within its boundaries lie four communities whose economies depend on commercial logging. Also within its boundaries are four Indian reservations, and they also depend on commercial logging for a lot of their income.

Directly to the east of the Olympic National Park Coastal Strip, which is administered by the U.S. National Park Service, are many privately held areas of land. These are owned and operated mostly by timber companies, and many of them contain stands of old-growth and late-successional second-growth trees. Some areas have been clear cut. Some areas have been reseeded.

Also to the east of the Olympic National Park Coastal Strip are several areas of land managed by other federal agencies, such as the Bureau of Land Management, the U.S. Forest Service, and the U.S. Fish and Wildlife Service. While all of these areas—including the Olympic National Park Coastal Strip—are managed by the federal government, they all serve different public purposes. Some are used for public recreation, some are leased to logging companies. Others are leased to mining companies, and still others are preserved as habitat to protect the biological species they contain.

Recently, a scientific panel presented the United States Congress and the President of the United States with evidence that all these different areas of forested land should be brought together under one land-use plan. The scientists concluded that all the different ecosystems are ecologically interconnected and, if one or more of them is deforested, then all the others will be adversely affected.

By law the U.S. Government is required to hold public hearings when it considers adopting a new land-use plan. Any land-use plan the government adopts must achieve a balance between ecological and economic factors. This is so that neither the biological species that rely on the forest for their habitat needs nor the humans who rely on the forest for their livelihoods will suffer.

Presiding over these hearings will be Judge Smith (your teacher), and it's your job to present Judge Smith with science-based evidence for considering and possibly adopting your group's land-use proposal. You will be working against a deadline, and other groups with other objectives will also be gathering scientific evidence to support their own proposals. First you must agree within your group on your objectives, and decide what kind of evidence you will need to support your objectives. Then you must conduct research to gather information and compile data. Finally, you will develop a land-use proposal based on your research.

As you think about your objectives and compile supporting data, you should keep in mind that other groups are engaged in the same process. Most likely, not everyone will agree on one particular group's land-use proposal, and the final land-use plan will probably contain elements from all the groups' proposals. So it's a good idea to start thinking about what other groups might want as you gather your own supporting data and develop your own proposal. Ultimately, all the groups are going to have to get together and reach an agreement on one plan. Here is a brief outline of the four groups that will be engaged in this process.

The Xylem Timber Company owns many hectares of forested land east of the Olympic National Park Coastal Strip, and they've used various harvesting techniques to extract timber over the past several decades. They currently practice sustained-yield forest management techniques on much of their land, because that's the best way to ensure that their stockholders continue to earn money.

SaveOlympic is a consortium of environmental groups that wants to preserve as much of the Olympic Peninsula's old-growth forest ecosystem as possible. They have been actively and publicly campaigning for the preservation of American natural resources since the 1970s, and their track record is pretty good. Recently, for example, they helped create a land-use plan that provides for the preservation of several hundred hectares of Louisiana bayou.

The President of the United States has instructed the various federal agencies that manage land in the Olympic Peninsula to work together to create a land-use proposal that addresses the concerns of many different interest groups. As a result, members of the National Park Service, the Forest Service, the Bureau of Land Management, and the Fish and Wildlife Service are working to put together a proposal that will best serve the public interest.

The Native Americans who live on the four Indian Reservations in the Olympic Peninsula have joined together because they are concerned about how deforestation has been affecting their salmon fisheries, which are a major source of their communities' income. Many of them also have jobs with the Xylem Timber Company. They want to make sure that their children are able to support themselves in the region.

These are the four groups from which Judge Smith will be hearing proposals. You will find more information about your own particular group on your Student Role sheet. As you work through this activity, remember that your ultimate goal is agreement, and agreement often involves compromise. Good luck!

Resources List

NSTA Publications

NSTA has published the following books on subjects related to the Global Change Series. For publication sales, call (800) 722-NSTA (U.S. & Canada). For general information, call (703) 243-7100. NSTA's home page is http://www.nsta.org.

National Science Teachers Association. *Global Environmental Change: Biodiversity.* Grades 9-12, 1997, 64 pp., #PB138X01.

Scripps Institution of Oceanography. *Forecasting the Future: Exploring Evidence for Global Climate Change.* Grades 6–10, 1996, 160 pp., #PB118X.

Ford, B. and Smith, P.S. *Project Earth Science: Meteorology.* Grades 5–10, 1994, 234 pp., #PB103X.

Understanding Our Environment. Grades 5–9, 1995, Seven-book set, #PB115X.

NSTA Marketed Publications

NSTA's Science Store markets the following books on related subjects produced by other publishers. This list is subject to change; contact NSTA for further information.

International Council of Scientific Unions. *Global Change.* Grades 10–college, 1994, 320 pp., #OP463X.

Ohio Sea Grant Education Program. *Great Lakes Instructional Materials for the Changing Earth System: Integrative Activities on Global Change.* Grades 5–12, 1995, 203 pp., #MS240X.

Roa, Michael L. *Environmental Science Activities Kit.* Grades 7–12, 1993, 330 pp., #OP283X.

The Science Teacher

The Science Teacher is NSTA's award winning professional journal for teachers in grades 7–12. This monthly publication features articles written by educators on a wide range of scientific topics, innovative teaching ideas and experiments, and current research news. *The Science Teacher* is one of many benefits of NSTA membership. For membership information, call (800) 830-3232 (U.S. & Canada) or 703-243-7100. The following articles from *The Science Teacher* articles relate to this publication:

Eichman, Julia and Jeff A. Brown. "Global Warming?" April 1994, pp. 24–28.

Hassard, Jack and Julie Weisburg. "The Global Thinking Project." April 1992, pp. 42–47.

Singletary, Ted J. and J. Richard Jordan. "Exploring the GLOBE." March 1996, pp. 36–39.

Books & Articles

Botkin, D.B. 1993. *Forest Dynamics: An Ecological Model.* New York: Oxford University Press.

Demchik, M.J. 1994. *Constructivism in Chemistry: A Global Issues Approach Resource Book.* Shenandoah, WV: Jefferson High School.

Golley, Frank B. (ed.). 1977. "Ecological Succession," in *Benchmark Papers in Ecology/5.* Stroudsburg, PA: Dowden, Hutchinson and Ross.

Hanson, E, Hays, D., Hicks, L., Young, L., and J. Buchanan. 1993. "Spotted Owl Habitat in Washington: A Report to the Washington Forest Practices Board." Olympia, WA: Washington Forest Practices Board Spotted Owl Advisory Committee.

Houghton, John. 1994. *Global Warming: The Complete Briefing.* Oxford, UK: Lion Publishing.

Leopold, Aldo. 1966. *A Sand County Almanac.* New York: Oxford University Press.

Miller, G. Tyler. 1994. *Living in the Environment: Principles, Connections, and Solutions.* Belmont, CA: Wadsworth, Inc.

United Nations Environmental Programme (UNEP). 1994. *Agenda 21: the United Nations Programme of Action from Rio.* New York: UNEP Environmental Library.

United Nations Environmental Programme (UNEP). 1993. *Global Biodiversity.* New York: UNEP Environmental Library.

U.S. Department of Agriculture. 1994. *Viability Assessments and Management Considerations for Species Associated with Late-Successional and Old-Growth Forests of the Pacific Northwest: The Report of the Scientific Analysis Team.* Washington, D.C.: U.S. Government Printing Office.

U.S. Environmental Protection Agency. 1994. *Record of Decision for Amendments to Forest Service and Bureau of Land Management Planning Documents Within the Range of the Northern Spotted Owl.* Washington, D.C.: U.S. Government Printing Office.

U.S. Department of the Interior, National Biological Service. 1995. *Our Living Resources: A Report to the Nation on the Distribution, Abundance, and Health of U.S. Plants, Animals, and Ecosystems.* Washington, D.C.: U.S. Government Printing Office.

Wilson, E.O. 1988. *Biodiversity.* Washington, D.C.: National Academy Press.

Curriculum

GLOBE Program
 744 Jackson Place
 Washington, D.C. 20503
 Tel.: (800) 858-9947
 email: help@globe.gov
 http://www.globe.gov

The Green Disk
 P.O. Box 32224
 Washington, D.C. 20007
 Tel.: (800) 484-7616
 Email: greendisk@igc.apc.org
 http://www.igc.org/greendisk

Wild Louisiana
 Louisiana Sea Grant Communications Office
 Louisiana State University
 Baton Rouge, LA 70803-7507
 http://www.lsu.edu/guests/wwwosgd

Websites

Canadian Forests
 http://www.canadian-forests.com/

Directory to Government Environmental Agencies
 http://www.studorg.nwu.edu/seed/envirogov.html

Earthviewer
 http://www.fourmilab.ch/earthview/vplanet.html

Environmental Organizations Web Directory
 http://www.webdirectory.com/

Organizations

American Forests
P.O. Box 2000
Washington, D.C. 20013
Tel.: 1-800-368-5748 or (202) 667-3300
http://www.amfor.org

Aspen Global Change Institute
100 East Francis Street
Aspen, CO 81611
Tel.: (970) 925-7376
Fax: (970) 925-7097
Email: agcimail@agci.org
http://www.gcrio.org/agci-home.html

Conservation International
1015 18th Street NW
Suite 100
Washington, D.C. 20036
Tel.: (800) 406-2306 or (202) 429-5660
http://www.conservation.org

Forest History Society, Inc.
701 Vickers Avenue
Durham, NC 27701
Tel.: (919) 682-9319
E-mail: coakes@acpub.duke.edu

Instituto Nacional de Biodiversidad (INBIO)
22-3100 Santo Domingo de Heredia
Heredia, Costa Rica

The Nature Conservancy
1815 N. Lynn Street
Arlington, VA 22209
Tel.: (800) 628-6860 or (703) 841-5300
http://www.tnc.org

Missouri Botanical Garden
P.O. Box 299
St. Louis, MO 63166-0299
Tel.: (314) 577-5100
http://www.mobot.org

World Resources Institute
1709 New York Avenue N.W.
7th Floor
Washington, D.C. 20006
Tel.: (202) 638-6300
http://www.wri.org

Forestry Companies & Associations

American Forest & Paper Association
1111 19th St. N.W., Suite 800
Washington, DC 20036
Tel.: (202) 463-2700
Fax: (202) 463-2785
Email:
INFO@afandpa.ccmail.compuserve.com
http://www.afandpa.org

California Forestry Association
300 Capitol Mall, Suite 350
Sacramento, CA 95814
Tel.: (916) 444-6592
Fax: (916) 444-0170
Email: cfa@cwo.com
http://www.foresthealth.org

California Forest Products Commission
2150 River Plaza Drive, #S-270
Sacramento, CA 95833
Tel.: (916) 568-1141
Fax: (916) 568-1144

Canadian Pulp and Paper Association
1155 Metcalfe St., 19th floor
Montreal, Quebec
Canada H3B 4T6
Tel: (514) 866-6621
Fax: (514) 866-3935
Email: calme@cam.org
http://www.portes.ouvertes.cppa.ca

Canadian Wood Council
1730 St. Laurent Blvd., Suite 350
Ottawa, Ontario
Canada K1G 5L1
http://www.cwc.metrics.com/cwc.html

Georgia Pacific Corporation
133 Peachtree St. N.E.
Atlanta, GA 30303
Phone: (404) 652-4000
http://www.gapac.com

Weyerhaeuser Company
http://www.weyerhaeuser.com

Government Agencies

Bureau of Land Management
Office of Public Affairs
1849 C Street, Room 504-LS
Washington, DC 20240
Tel.: (202) 452-5125
http://www.blm.gov

Environment Canada
Inquiry Center
Place Vincent Massey
351 St. Joseph's Blvd.
Hull, Quebec
Canada K1A OH3
Tel.: (819) 997-2800
http://www.doe.ca

National Oceanic and Atmospheric
Administration (NOAA)
NOAA Correspondence Unit
1305 East West Highway
Room 8624
Silver Spring, MD 20910
Email: opca@esdim.noaa.gov
http://www.noaa.gov

National Weather Service
1325 East-West Highway
Silver Spring, MD 20910
Tel.: 301-713-0689
http://www.nws.noaa.gov

Natural Resources Conservation Service
1400 Independence Avenue SW
Washington, DC 20250
Tel.: (202) 720-2791
http://www.ncg.nrcs.usda.gov

United Nations Environmental Programme
Chief, Office of the Executive Director
PO Box 30552
Nairobi, Kenya
Phone: (254) 2 621234
Fax: (254) 2 226890 or 215787
Email: oedinfo@unep.org
http://www.unep.no

U.S. Department of Agriculture
1400 Independence Ave. SW
Washington, D.C. 20250
Tel.: (202) 720-2791
http://www.usda.gov

U.S. Department of the Interior
1849 C Street, NW
Washington, D.C. 20240
Tel.: (202) 208-3100
http://www.doi.gov

U.S. Environmental Protection Agency
401 M Street, SW
Washington, D.C. 20460
Tel.: (202) 260-2090
http://www.epa.gov

U.S. Fish and Wildlife Service
Reference Service
5430 Grosvenor Lane, Suite 110
Bethesda, MD 20814-2142
Tel.: (800) 582-3421 or (301) 492-6403
Fax: 301-564-4059
http://www.fws.gov

U.S. Forest Service
P.O. Box 96090
Washington, D.C. 20090
Tel.: (202) 205-1760
http://www.fs.fed.us

U.S. Geological Survey
12201 Sunrise Valley Drive
Reston, VA 20192, USA
Tel.: 703-648-4000
http://www.usgs.gov

U.S. Global Change Research Information
Office
GCRIO User Services
2250 Pierce Road
Universit y Center, MI 48710
Tel.: (517) 797-2730
Fax: (517) 797-2622
Email: help@gcrio.org
http://www.gcrio.org

U.S. National Park Service
1849 C Street, NW
Washington, DC 20240
Tel.: (202) 208-4747
http://www.nps.gov

TEACHER NOTES

Global Environmental Change: Biodiversity

Biodiversity uses Costa Rica as a case study in balancing economic growth and resource conservation. The volume introduces students to basic scientific themes and equips them with tools to increase their understanding of biodiversity. Cumulative, teacher-tested, hands-on classroom activities teach students how to integrate science with other disciplines, to gather information, and make decisions toward solving problems. *Biodiversity* is the first book in a *Global Environmental Change* series created by NSTA and the U.S. Environmental Protection Agency. The series covers topics ranging from biological diversity to deforestation to solid waste management.
Grades 9-12, 1997, 64 pp.   **#PB138X01**

Forecasting the Future

Is the Earth's climate changing? What could global climate change ? *Forecasting the Future: Exploring Evidence for Global Climate Change* cuts through the confusion to address this vital issue in a scientific manner. Developed with Scripps Institution of Oceanography, this volume features background information that examines past and potential climatic changes. Fourteen classroom activities and more than 40 extension exercises help students understand climate change through animal biology, chemistry, geology, meteorology, physics, and plant biology. The concepts are tied together by a sophisticated timeline that illustrates climate change, major extinctions, and other key events.
Grades 6-10, 1996, 160 pp.   **#PB118X**

Explore the World Using Protozoa

Protozoa may not be the first things that come to mind when you think of adaptation, evolution, food webs, colonization, succession, physiology and morphology, or life strategies. But these microorganisms are a great tool to model these and other scientific concepts, principles, and processes because protozoa perform many of the same activities seen in their macroscopic counterparts. And they are much easier to cultivate and maintain in the classroom. This book's 28 teacher-tested, hands-on investigations will help you teach organizing principles of biology and ecology and make links to other disciplines.
Grades 9-College, 1996, 240 pp.   **#PB137X**

Water Matters, Volume II

This second volume in NSTA's popular *Water Matters* series focuses on the ground water and water quality. The packet includes a 32-page written teacher's guide as well as elementary and middle-level editions of USGS posters on Navigation, Ground Water, and Water Quality. Sort through dozens of activities and extensions to find hands-on learning experiences perfect for your classes. Teachers can use this book for introductory purposes or as a detailed curriculum unit on water education. The book is a great complement to Water Matters Volume I, which covers wetlands, water use, and wastewater treatment.
Grades 3-8, 1997, 32 pp.   **#PB116X2**

National Science Teachers Association

To order, or for a free catalog, call: 1-800-722-NSTA or fax 703-522-6091
Visit the NSTA web site at http://www.nsta.org or email pubsales@nsta.org

Deforestation

ALSO FROM NSTA

NSTA: Committed to Science Education Excellence

The National Science Teachers Association is the world's largest organization dedicated to improving science education on all levels—preschool through college. NSTA promotes this goal through a range of professional activities.

A Dedication to Excellence

Membership in NSTA brings educators into a vibrant organization of more than 53,000 science teachers, science supervisors, administrators, scientists, business and industry representatives, and others representing every facet of science education. NSTA conducts national and regional conventions that attract more than 30,000 attendees annually.

NSTA provides a variety of programs and services for science educators, including awards, professional development workshops, and educational tours. The association is active in promoting the National Science Education Standards. NSTA's "Building a Presence for Science" seeks to align science teaching with the standards in every school in the nation.

Special Publications

NSTA's Special Publication Division publishes books and other media on all key topics and disciplines in science education—including global environmental change, the science of HIV, Earth science, classroom assessment, chemistry, physics, and space science.

NSTA members receive notification about the publication of new NSTA books. Members also receive a 10 percent discount on all publications in NSTA's *Membership & Publications Catalog*, which includes more than 200 specially-chosen titles. The association provides free copies of the catalog and the *Supplement of Science Education Suppliers* to its membership.

Journals & Periodicals

NSTA is a major publisher of materials for educators. NSTA members choose from among four journals, each for a specific grade level: *Science and Children* (elementary), *Science Scope* (middle level), *The Science Teacher* (high school), and *Journal of College Science Teaching* (college). NSTA journals feature lively, "how to do it" articles, commentary, research, colorful posters, and monthly columns.

Two NSTA magazines designed for students, parents, and teachers—*Dragonfly* and *Quantum*—are available by subscription. *Dragonfly* is designed for use in grades 3–6. *Quantum*, which focuses on math and science, offers feature articles, olympiad-style problems, and brainteasers. NSTA's newspaper, *NSTA Reports!*, features news on education issues, teaching resources, funding opportunities, and more.

Membership Benefits

◆ Award-winning periodicals

◆ Deep discounts for conventions and other activities

◆ Advance notice of NSTA conventions, conferences, and publications

◆ Access to over 30 awards

◆ Certification programs for teachers in elementary through high school

◆ Group rate insurance plans

◆ Voting privileges for individuals

Popular NSTA Titles

◆ *Project Earth Science*: series, including *Astronomy, Geology, Meteorology, & Oceanography*

◆ *Views of the Solar System CD-ROM*

◆ *Pathways to the National Science Education Standards*

◆ *Craters! A Multi-Science Guide to Cratering & Impacts*

◆ *The Science of HIV*

NSTA Journals & Periodicals

◆ *Science & Children (elementary)*

◆ *Science Scope (middle level)*

◆ *The Science Teacher (high school)*

◆ *Journal of the College Science Teacher (college)*

◆ *Dragonfly (students in grades 3-6, by subscription)*

◆ *Quantum: The Magazine of Math and Science (students, by subscription)*

◆ *NSTA Reports (6 times annually)*

Address: 1840 Wilson Blvd., Arlington, VA 22201-3000 USA
Telephone: 1-800-830-3232 (Membership); 1-800-722-NSTA (Publication Sales, North America); 703-243-7100 (Main Number)
Email: membership@nsta.org (Membership); pubsales@nsta.org (Publication Sales); spubs@nsta.org (Special Publications Editorial)
World Wide Web: http://www.nsta.org